FINDING YOUR PATHWAY TO BELONGING IN EDUCATION

DR. ILENE WINOKUR

EduMatch
PUBLISHING

ISBN: 978-1-959347-13-2

CONTENTS

ABOUT THIS BOOK

Pathways to Belonging in Education is a companion book to my first book, *Journey to Belonging: Pathways to Well-being,* and a guide for teachers who need to support their students' self-belonging and personal belonging while supporting their own self-belonging and professional belonging. This workbook can be used to enrich your lesson planning by creating a sense of safety and belonging in your classroom. It is filled with lessons and activities created by educators like you—amazing educators I am lucky to have in my professional learning network (PLN). This book can be used without reading my first book, *Journey to Belonging: Pathways to Well-Being,* but it will be more useful if you understand the background behind the different types of belonging that are discussed in more detail there.

Feel free to use, modify, and share the ideas in this book with other educators. You will find links and QR codes throughout the book with additional resources and information.

ACKNOWLEDGMENTS

This book would not be possible without the contributions of educators I am so lucky to learn with and from. I encourage you to follow them on social media or look at their websites to find out more.

Barbara Bray
Twitter: bbray27
Website: https://barbarabray.net

Dr. Denise Furlong
Twitter: denise_furlong

Melisa Hayes
Twitter: MrsHayesfam

Rola Tbshirani
Twitter: rolat

Dr. Carol Salva
Twitter: DrCarolSalva

Tan Huynh
Twitter: TanKHuynh

Kristina Holzweiss
Twitter: lieberrian
Website: https://www.bunheadwithducttape.com

Valentina Gonzalez
Twitter: ValentinaESL

Justin Garcia
Twitter: Kruu_Justin

Scott Nunes
Twitter: MrNunesteach

Noa Daniel
Twitter: iamnoadaniel
Website:https://buildingoutsidetheblocks.com

Melody McAllister
Twitter: mjmcalliwrites

Victoria Thompson
Twitter: VictoriaTheTech
https://sites.google.com/view/victoriathetech/home

Bhavna Mathew
Twitter: MathewBhavna

Mandy Froehlich
Twitter: FroehlichM
Website: https://www.mandyfroehlich.com

Justin Nolan
JustTries
Website: https://www.justtries.ca

Janique Caseley
Twitter: 6Caseley
https://sites.google.com/gnspes.ca/gradesixcaseley/home

INTRODUCTION

One of the major things I missed when I became an administrator was teaching a classroom filled with students. Even more than being physically present with students, I missed planning and innovating my lessons. Over the past few years, I have learned a number of apps and edtech tools that I wished existed when I was teaching ten years ago. Tools like Flip (formerly Flipgrid), Buncee, Wakelet, Book Creator, Nearpod, Microsoft Teams, Google for Education, Belouga, Canva, and Adobe Creative Express have challenged my learning and enhanced my ability to communicate my message about belonging, inclusion, equity, compassion, and supporting refugees. Lately, I have seen the amazing things teachers are creating for their students to ensure learning continues even as we faced so much disruption and uncertainty during the pandemic. I realize how important it is to share what I've learned about creating a culture of safety and a place for everyone to feel a sense of belonging.

In 1996, I was working in an administrative office at Kuwait University. It was my first job in Kuwait since the first eleven years had been filled with raising my three children. I wasn't very excited about the work since it was mostly pushing papers, but I loved the team I was working with and had the chance to read and speak Arabic in a professional setting. About halfway through the first year, I received a call from a close friend who worked at my sons' school. We chatted for a bit about our kids and then she mentioned that one of the reading support teachers she worked with in the elementary school was leaving her job to become the superintendent at a new, all-girls school with an American curriculum. I kept thinking about our conversation. My friend had planted a seed that made me wonder about professional opportunities at the new school. Since I wasn't feeling fulfilled or motivated at my administrative job, I took the opportunity to find out if there were any teaching positions available at this new school.

After I spoke to Evelyn, the new school's superintendent, about my interest in becoming a teacher, she told me it was better if I didn't apply for first and second grade which were important years for basic skills since I didn't have a degree in education or any experience teaching other than providing support for my children when they needed help. I told her that I was willing to learn. She realized the advantage of hiring me since I am a native English speaker who could be hired on a local contract. This would save the school money since I wouldn't need an overseas teacher benefits package that included airfare and housing. Evelyn told me she wanted me to teach third grade. I was delighted! Since it was the inaugural year for the school, she also told me I'd be the only teacher in that grade level since the owners weren't sure how many students would register.

As soon as I signed the contract to start in September 1996, I realized I needed to start researching and learning about teaching third-grade-level English language learners using an American curriculum. I was delighted about having the opportunity to start a new career and also become a learner again.

Initially, I confess I was attracted to teaching because of the summer vacation schedule which meant I could travel with my husband and children to visit my family in the U.S. I was also happy to have a job that challenged me to learn something new since I didn't have the education or experience to teach with my bachelor's degree in history and my M.B.A. in finance. The first organization I discovered was ASCD (formerly the Association for Supervision and Curriculum Development). Education experts like Carol Ann Tomlinson and Grant Wiggins were providing professional development in the area of differentiated education and a focus on starting where the students are and then building their skills. I learned so much from the articles and books I received with my membership! Eventually, I had the opportunity to attend the ASCD annual conference. I took advantage of every session related to my areas of interest and the presentations on teaching English learners. When I returned to Kuwait, I had research-based methods and strategies to support the learners in my class and around my school.

The school opened with 85 students and 20 teachers and staff. There was only one class per grade level (Pre-K to grade 5 the first year), except for the kindergarten which had two sections each. Every day I came home from work and my husband would ask me, "Are you going to have a job next year? Will the school stay open?" I calmly told him that the parents were satisfied and I was sure there would be a higher enrollment the following year. There were eight students in my third-grade class and one of them spoke no English at all. This was problematic since we used an American curriculum and books in English. I did my best to accommodate her language deficit by allowing her to draw her answers and receiving some help from her peers in her home language, Arabic, if she had no idea what we were saying. At that point, I was fairly fluent in Arabic but I didn't let the students know until they were already into a routine of using English in the classroom. The first time they realized I understood them, they were so surprised!

This was my first year as a teacher and I knew that my professional development in second language acquisition and pedagogy was essential if my students were going to succeed. I searched online for research and advice about teaching second language learners and classroom management. I realized early on there were vast differences in the language and learning abilities of my students. I knew I needed to differentiate my lessons to accommodate my students' learning levels and needs. This led me to Carol Ann Tomlinson's differentiated instruction.

While learning more about teaching English language learners, I realized I needed to modify my lesson plans to ensure my students were seeing the connections between their learning and how to apply it. This prompted me to explore different activities that would fill in gaps they had in basic skills and knowledge. For example, there was a unit in their social studies book about the Revolutionary War in America. I knew this was going to be difficult for them to relate to, so I divided up the chapter according to how challenging the passages were, put the students into groups of the same reading level, and assigned passages accordingly to their level (jigsaw method). Then I told them they must teach the other students their part of the chapter by acting it out and then quizzing their classmates to see if they understood it. The results were amazing! I gave them time to work on it in class, and then each group presented it to the others and quizzed them. I was there to guide them and make sure they covered the main ideas.

I also modeled good reading skills for the students by reading aloud and doing "think alouds." This method is terrific for second language learners (and all students for that matter). First, I read the entire paragraph out loud. Then I read it a second time, and as I read, I told them what I was thinking. For example, if I came upon a difficult word, I would stop and talk about what it meant, using common reading strategies: within the context of the other sentences, or looking at prefix/suffix, or a root word they already knew. After I did this a few times, I asked students to volunteer and try it. I also told them if they were stumped, to look the word up in the dictionary as a last resort.

The more I researched, the more I learned. In my first two years of teaching, I discovered that my lesson plans were not supporting the way I taught. I needed to see the big picture (standards and objectives) before I could relate my lessons to the student learning outcomes. Instead of starting with the textbook or activity, I began connecting the teaching standards and student outcomes with the content. I discovered Grant Wiggins' and Jay McTighe's *Understanding by Design,* and it all clicked! I began using a lesson plan designed backward. I unpacked the standards, created big idea questions, focused on the assessment, and lastly, designed the activity. The lesson plan template I used has been modified for use in this book. You will find most of the lessons or activities in this book have been formatted using this template.

Feel free to use the template below since it's widely available from educators and districts that follow the backward design. On the next page is a blank template to help you get started.

TOPIC

CREATED BY:

STANDARD(S)/OBJECTIVE(S)	LEARNING OUTCOME(S)

CONNECTION TO BELONGING

OVERARCHING/DRIVING QUESTION	ASSESSMENT

ACTIVITY

HOW TO USE THIS BOOK

Pathways to Belonging is divided into sections that align with the types of belonging mentioned in my 2021 book, *Journey to Belonging: Pathways to Well-Being*: self-belonging, personal belonging, professional belonging, and becoming a good ancestor. In addition, the first section provides suggestions for creating a safe and welcoming environment in your classroom to ensure students feel a sense of belonging.

Note: Although this workbook/guide is meant as a companion book to *Journeys to Belonging*, those who haven't purchased it can still make full use of this book based on the explanations and additional resources I am providing. At the beginning of each section, there is a short explanation of the type of belonging and some additional information for context. You will also find a few links to additional resources at the end of the book.

You will see that each lesson or activity is formatted in a table that follows "backward design"[1] principles. The goal or outcome is first, then the lesson or activity's relationship to belonging, followed by overarching or essential question(s), assessment suggestions (if applicable), and finally, a description of the lesson or activity. Some of the lessons/activities include links. These will also be available as QR codes. Some lessons or activities will include a shortlist of content vocabulary. This list is to ensure maximum understanding of the task or project, inclusivity, and access by all students, whatever their learning needs.

I'd like to thank all of the educators who contributed lessons and activities to this book. Be sure to give them proper recognition if you use their ideas.

Some activities may seem to be at a higher or lower level than your students. Most can be modified to suit the needs of the grade or age level you are teaching.

CREATING A SAFE AND WELCOMING ENVIRONMENT FOR ALL

The first step to instilling a sense of belonging in students is your classroom environment. To feel a sense of belonging, students need to feel safe, physically and psychologically. Therefore, your students must have routines, an awareness of teacher and school expectations, and establish trusting relationships with their teachers and peers.

Greeting students at the door of your classroom is a wonderful signal to students that they matter to you. They see that you have put aside whatever else you have to do and you're focused on each of them.

Establishing class norms is something each teacher should prioritize on the first day of school. It immediately creates a classroom environment that validates individual participation and collaboration using guidelines created by the teacher who facilitates the discussion and guides students through the process. Norms should be posted in an easily viewed/accessible part of the classroom for all to see and refer to throughout the year. Norms can be modified or discussion opened again if there is any change or need during the year.[1]

Video of classroom norms (Edutopia)

CLASS NORMS

CREATED BY DR. ILENE WINOKUR

STANDARD(S)/OBJECTIVE(S)

*Group norms are necessary for improved classroom management and learning.
*Each person in the classroom is aware of expectations and learning is enhanced.

LEARNING OUTCOME(S)

*Students will be able to distinguish between norms and rules.
*Students will be aware of their individual responsibilities and behavior and how it contributes to a safe and welcoming environment in their classroom to maximize learning.

CONNECTION TO BELONGING

In order to instill a sense of belonging, the classroom must first be a safe space. Safe, in this sense means psychological and physical safety. Class norms are established by consensus and collaboration, with a focus on respect, inclusivity, and acceptance.

OVERARCHING/DRIVING QUESTION

*In communities, why are there norms or expectations of behavior that support individual rights and responsibility towards others' rights?
*Why is it important to come to a consensus about the norms rather than having them imposed by someone else?
*How can we, as a class community, ensure students' individual rights to learn and express themselves while ensuring the rights of all are respected?

ASSESSMENT

*Students can create a poll or survey to gauge the level of safety they feel after the norms are agreed to and have been in a place for several weeks.
    Do students feel heard and seen?
    Do students feel comfortable speaking in class?

ACTIVITY

*Using whole group and/or small group discussion, students create a short (4–6) list of class norms that each student and the teacher agree to follow.
*Content vocabulary: norm, consensus, rights, responsibilities, expectations

Note: Norm is the preferred word to use rather than "rules" since norm implies consensus while rule implies something imposed.

We often hear recommendations from teachers to stand in their doorways and greet students each morning or during the class period. The importance of this cannot be overstated. If you're on social media, you've probably seen posts (mostly pre-pandemic) of teachers high-fiving or doing different handshakes with each of their students as they enter the classroom. Juxtapose these with a teacher sitting at their desk, looking at their lesson plan or computer, not looking up at any of the students until the bell rings and class starts. If our students were guests in our home, we would definitely not ignore them when they arrived. We would greet them warmly and make them feel comfortable. We'd ask them how they were feeling and what was new in their lives. The signal we give our students if we are sitting at our desks immersed in our work, no matter how urgent, is that they don't matter. If we're trying to create a welcoming space in our classrooms, everything counts, including how we meet and greet our students. In fact, we should be meeting them from the time they enter the school and not waiting for them to walk all the way to our classrooms. This doesn't change no matter what grade level or age. Relationships matter and are one important way to create the setting for relationships, trust, and safety.

That leads me to the next area we must be aware of which are safe spaces in our schools and classrooms. Safety includes physical and psychological safety without the threat of bullying or othering. All of us, teachers, staff, administrators, and students, must feel they are heard and seen and they are valued and accepted for being their authentic selves. Nobody should have to "hide" their identity because of their appearance, beliefs, or background. Schools should be welcome to all who enter, and they should feel welcome and respected.

Administrators, staff, and teachers should model the behaviors we expect from our students such as how we talk to and about each other and our students. One example from my own experience is a student who had a behavior problem according to her previous teachers. In 2010, I was hired by a local private university in Kuwait to teach Level 2 English in an intensive English program. I already had an understanding of the nuances of the Arabic language and believed I could use that knowledge to inform how I would teach pre-college students with weak academic English skills. I was new to the age group, but not new to teaching ESL. I planned my lessons for the first week of class and looked forward to meeting my students. In the hallway outside of my office, teachers were exchanging the names of those who were registered in their sections. It seemed that when I mentioned one particular student's name, the reaction was the same each time. "Uh oh!! You need to be careful of HER." Last semester, she tried to get her teacher fired. She's a real problem. Be very careful." I can continue with the story and tell you that I didn't listen to the previous teachers and their dire warnings, but I want to focus on the fact that the teachers were speaking in the hallway about a particular student. This happened on several occasions when I was walking to my office and passed by teachers sharing their experiences and using very negative language to describe how they felt about the student. The hallways often had students walking to different offices and they could have overheard things like, "You know how lazy these students are; so and so doesn't come to class and when he does, he expects me to accept his excuses...." You get the idea. If we are going to model behavior, this isn't the way to do it. And this deficit-based attitude is a mindset toward the student. It shows me that the teacher hasn't asked or tried to find out the reason for the student's misbehavior.

Another easy yet important way to show students you care by creating a safe space is daily or regular check-ins. There are many ways to do this. [2]

Some quick examples:

- Get to know them really well as soon as possible at the start of the year.
- Create relationships with students by letting them know you value them and take the time to validate their thoughts, ideas, and feelings.
- Respect that they might not want to share or tell their story.
- Share our big feelings through storytelling; for example, have them think of a time that they felt overwhelmed (or describe a character in a story whether in English or another language).

In order to come back to feeling calm, we need to define our feelings and move forward. Little things like extending the wait time after a question is posed goes a long way to reducing anxiety about answering incorrectly.

Welcoming Students With a Smile (Edutopia)

LESSON PLANNING AND INSTILLING A SENSE OF BELONGING

Normally when we think about lesson planning, we concentrate on teaching objectives connected to the curriculum's content. However, if we plan with the intention of reaching all of our students, we also need to add language and culture objectives. Language objectives, as well as culture objectives, are useful for intentional lesson planning and support language learners as well as other students.

I recently heard about culture objectives from Dr. José Medina in a short reel on Instagram. When I searched online to find out more, I found a blog post by Tan Huynh, a contributor to this book and an English language specialist who also learned about culture objectives from Dr. Medina. Huyhn writes,

The goal of a culture objective is to connect students' lived experiences and backgrounds to the content, positively reflect students' cultures within the curriculum, and expand their linguistic repertoire.

He notes that Dr. Medina "suggests four ways teachers can use to write culture objectives.

1. Amplify the voices of marginalized communities
2. Connect to the child and/or the real world
3. Encourage cross-linguistic connections and translanguaging
4. Present social and academic language as equals"[1]

How to Write Language and Culture Objectives (Tan Huyhn)

Teaching diverse literature is an example of a lesson that integrates the three types of objectives: content, language, and culture. When resources for learning are books, poems, or prose that reflect students' experiences and connect to their stories, we ensure that students feel "seen." Using a variety of picture books at any grade level is a great way to prompt discussion, as well as be more inclusive and culturally responsive. When children see themselves in the content and literature, they make connections to their own lives and this lowers the affective filter (see p. 52 for a full explanation).

An example of a lesson that uses language and culture objectives is *Is it HIS-tory or Our Story?* The lesson begins on the next page.

Note that culture objectives do not have to be written, but they should be decided on and kept in mind as the lesson or unit is being developed.

IS IT HIS-TORY OR OUR STORY?

CREATED BY: DR. ILENE WINOKUR

STANDARD(S)/OBJECTIVE(S)

Look at different events in history (based on your curriculum) from various perspectives. Search for various articles, books, poems, etc. that represent many sides of lived stories during the period you're studying.

LEARNING OUTCOME(S)

*Students will learn about a period in history from different perspectives through lived narratives, experiences, and reports of the time. Example: Civil Rights Movement 1960s America

CONNECTION TO BELONGING

Perspective-taking is directly related to empathy and compassion for others. It also allows us to see within ourselves and how we view situations.

LANGUAGE OBJECTIVE(S)

Choose keywords based on the content that students need to understand that will support their comprehension. If you are using a variety of readings, choose a few keywords for each reading or as necessary.

CULTURE OBJECTIVES()

Present the content from all perspectives by being inclusive, amplifying voices, connecting to the child and the real world, validating different points of view.

OVERARCHING/DRIVING QUESTION(S)

Why are there different interpretations of history?
How does who is writing the story affect how the story is told?
How can we be sure we understand all sides of an issue?

ASSESSMENT

*A project idea would be to find a variety of sources from a time period and role-play, create a play, or comic strip, etc. that portrays the different perspectives given by each of the sources.

ACTIVITY

Students choose an event in history or from the time period being studied in class and depict how the people who lived at the time perceived and remembered the event.

AN ASSET-BASED APPROACH TO TEACHING

We often hear about people who either believe the glass is half empty or half full. Have you ever heard that a glass can be refilled? How does changing our perception from a deficit mindset (glass half-empty) to an asset-based mindset (glass can be refilled) improve how we perceive our students and how they perceive themselves? What is an asset-based approach to education? The Steinhardt School of Education at New York University[1] notes,

> It focuses on strengths. It views diversity in thought, culture, and traits as positive assets. Teachers and students alike are valued for what they bring to the classroom rather than being characterized by what they may need to work on or lack.

An Asset-Based Approach to Education (NYU article, 2018)

Being "seen" in the literature and recognizing topics learned in their home language can go a long way in connecting students to the content and to learning English. When I began teaching grade 3 in Kuwait, the whole class was learning English. The school followed an American curriculum so the textbooks were published in the U.S. Examples of cultural dissonance included math: the currency (dollars) and the measurement system (imperial versus metric) were very confusing to the students. In social studies, they were learning about the American Revolution and other events they couldn't relate to. Rather than teaching them the essential vocabulary and concepts, I planned my lessons intentionally. I created manipulatives of dollars and cents along with dinars and fils (Kuwait's currency). Students used the money to plan a pizza party and had to be sure they stayed within a budget. The concept of a single currency was emphasized and how many cents add up to a dollar rather than the name of the currency. We measured using both systems, but I emphasized the key vocabulary (inches, feet), and we walked around the school measuring different objects and rooms. We discussed the basic differences between the measurement systems but focused more on the metric since that's what students knew. When we learned about the Revolutionary War, the students read about it and decided how to present the information they learned to the rest of the class. I scaffolded the reading from the textbook using the "jigsaw" method since it was above their level of comprehension. Each small group of students was responsible for reading and explaining their passage to the rest of the students. They chose how to present it based on their interests; some reenacted it while others drew pictures to show.

Lowering our expectations of students or having a deficit mindset influences how students think of themselves. It's important to find ways to relate the content to their interests and strengths. That is an asset-based approach. Students feel comfortable and confident to explore a new language because learning it is meaningful. According to a recent article by Jessica Villalobos for ASCD (2020)[2], "An asset-based approach to teaching English language learners is about creating a culture where we acknowledge strengths and expect success." Villalobos works in a district in New Mexico that supports many newcomers and language learners. Based on her own experience as an ELL, she is aware of the necessity for emphasizing her students' strengths and finding ways to ensure they are connecting with the content. Villalobos is an advocate for district-wide change and recommends several ways educators can support an asset-based approach including the use of culturally responsive literature, strategic scaffolding in all subjects, and focusing on student success by taking note of it.

An Asset-Based Approach to Support ELL Success (ASCD)

A few years ago, I was presenting at a private school in Kuwait. The language medium is English and the majority of students were Kuwaiti nationals whose first language was Arabic. I have often encountered a deficit mindset about language learners, so after introducing myself, I started the session with this query: "Raise your hand if you know the stages of second language acquisition." Of the 100 or so teachers in the room, only three raised their hands. Although I wasn't surprised, it disappointed me because teachers who don't have an understanding of how long it takes to learn a new language often become impatient with the slow process of learning. They don't realize that most students are taking the time they need to process the new vocabulary and express themselves in the target language. This leads to a deficit-based mindset which impacts how students think of themselves as learners. If they hear "you can't do it" and "your progress is slow" often enough, they will be convinced they are failures and can't learn English (or any other subject for that matter). I've had students in my classroom who told me they are 'bad' in English.

So, how can teachers and parents ensure children have a growth mindset? Below are five ways teachers and parents can help children grow their sense of self-belonging and increase their positive self-talk to help them become more confident learners.

Build Self-Belonging

1. Don't water down the content or lower expectations. Scaffold lessons, plan carefully and help children learn the skills needed to overcome the gaps in their learning.

2. Spend time finding out and then focusing on each child's strengths. (I call them superpowers). When opportunities arise to use their superpowers, notice them and celebrate how they use them to overcome challenges.

3. Build resilience and perseverance in children by using relatable literature or real-life examples from their own lives or others.

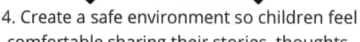

4. Create a safe environment so children feel comfortable sharing their stories, thoughts, and dreams. They will feel validated and valued.

5. Children who have an opportunity to use their voices and make choices become empowered learners. Voice and choice should be built into their daily lives in school and at home.

It's important for teachers to find a balance between discussing a student's superpowers and gaps in their learning. Students are more likely to achieve when we emphasize how their assets or strengths can be used to support their path to achieving learning outcomes and overcoming any gaps. The reason: it will have a positive impact on their self-image and self-perception.

LESSONS AND ACTIVITIES FOR SELF-BELONGING

Self-belonging is the composite of self-esteem, -efficacy, -confidence, -worth, -awareness: the sum total of a good self-concept. Having a sense of self-belonging eliminates self-doubt and negative self-talk. Encouraging each person, young and old, to have a voice, some choice, and ensuring ownership of tasks and decisions reinforces how each of us feels about ourselves. Having a sense of self-belonging increases the likelihood of healthy relationships with others.

In a guest blog post for *The Open Book Blog*, Katie Cunningham[1] describes how she, her children, and students react to prompts through literature and a documentary film about living to be happy by feeling a sense of belonging. Read more about it in her post.

Using Children's Books to Teach About Love and Belonging

RUMPLE BUTTERCUP

CREATED BY: DR. ILENE WINOKUR

STANDARD(S)/OBJECTIVE(S)

Create an inclusive classroom and a space where all students feel seen and heard.

LEARNING OUTCOME(S)

- Students will find parallels to the story, Rumple Buttercup, by Matthew Gray Gubler, in their own lives and be able to discuss their perception of themselves and how to overcome feelings of being different or weird.
- Students will consider what it is like to feel different or weird and how we can be more inclusive and accepting of others who might feel that way.

CONNECTION TO BELONGING

Our self-talk influences our perception of ourselves based on those around us. If we believe we're different or 'weird', our self-esteem is poor. This story shows us all that it doesn't matter if we aren't all the same.

OVERARCHING/DRIVING QUESTION(S)

What lessons can we learn from Rumple Buttercup about ourselves?
How can we feel better about being different?
How can we help others to feel less 'weird', more included?

ASSESSMENT

Create a rubric for whichever idea you use.
Have students role-play the story or write a script that shows they understand the themes and messages of the story.
Let students decide how they will be assessed.

ACTIVITY

Read aloud Rumple Buttercup, or purchase a class set of the book and have each student read it.
Stop at parts to discuss themes such as difference, inclusion, self-perception, acceptance, friendship, etc.
Have students journal how they're feeling about Rumple in different parts of the story.
Ask students to describe a time when they felt 'weird' or different. They can draw, write, role-play, use video or audio.

Ask these questions for discussion or create a list of these questions for students to respond to and let them choose how they want to respond.

- If Candycorn Carl was real, what would he be saying to Rumple? Write a conversation they might have.Why did Rumple feel like he was different? Why was he hiding in the sewer? What would you say to Rumple if you knew him?
- What did you think of Rumple's disguise (putting a banana peel on his head)?
- What do you think Rumple meant by "feeling normal" when he was above ground?
- What do you think "normal" is? ("Hidden under his banana peel, Rumple almost felt normal.")
- Story sequence: What happens at the beginning, middle, and end of the story?
- When Rumple finally realized he hadn't been hidden all those years, how did he feel?
- Describe a time when you helped someone feel like they belonged. What did you do or say?

DEAR ME

CREATED BY: DR. ILENE WINOKUR

STANDARD(S)/OBJECTIVE(S)	LEARNING OUTCOME(S)
*Learning how to share big feelings through storytelling *Personal improvement	*Students will learn about a period in history from different perspectives through lived narratives, experiences, and reports of the time. Example: Civil Rights Movement 1960s America

CONNECTION TO BELONGING

Chances for reflecting on our feelings and what's happening in our lives is rare. By journaling about your day, your feelings, or a specific event or occurrence, you spend time thinking about it more deeply. Reflection leads to better self-awareness which is the first step to feeling a sense of belonging.

OVERARCHING/DRIVING QUESTION(S)	ASSESSMENT
When we journal every day, we have a running record of our feelings and what has happened in our lives. How can we use storytelling to share our feelings and help us deal better with disappointments, trauma, and negative feelings?	*There are several ways to assess this depending on if it's a long-term project or short-term activity. *A rubric should be created and given to students before they start the activity and should list the skills that will be evaluated and how they will be assessed to guide self-assessment or to facilitate the creation of a final product that the teacher will assess. Note: If a longer-term project, a timeline with shorter deadlines should be handed out to students along with the rubric.

ACTIVITY

Watch the video (see QR code on p. 25) about values and identity. Then discuss it as a whole class. You can also make up a list of prompts or guiding questions for students to read through and reflect on as they watch or after they watch.

Once students have discussed and started to describe who they are, direct them to create a journal using their choice of modality or a combination of these: writing, drawing, photographing, audio or visual recordings, to represent their ideas about their identity. Then they create a portfolio of personal artifacts such as photos, drawings, writings, recordings, and words told to them about places and/or events that had an effect on how they view or feel about themselves.

A variety of apps like Wakelet, Buncee, Canva, and Adobe Express can be used in this activity and it can be extended over time to become a project or year-long activity. Wakelet can be used as a way to curate all of the students' reflections/journal entries.

Well-being for Children: Identity and Values (video)

WHAT'S IN A NAME (W.I.N.)

CREATED BY: NOA DANIEL

STANDARD(S)/OBJECTIVE(S)

Teachers can find writing, speaking, and/or SEL standards/objectives that align with this project.

LEARNING OUTCOME(S)

Students introduce themselves to their classmates and get to know themselves a bit better.

CONNECTION TO BELONGING

Students build a sense of belonging through this name–origin story.
Teachers give students the floor and time to share their projects with their class to increase class community.

OVERARCHING/DRIVING QUESTION

What's in a name (WIN)?
How do our names identify us AND become our identity?

ASSESSMENT

It is also a great diagnostic for presentation and research skills.
Link to outline and rubric:

ACTIVITY

Learners listen to each WIN presentation and get a wider view of their classmates. It's great for building and assessing presentation, research, and learning skills as students interview their parents on their name selection, explore the etymology of their names, who else shares it, and more.
For those unhappy with their name, students can propose one they wish they had been given. It's a Build Outside the Blocks (BOB) project that I share far and wide because it helps students learn about themselves while also building skill, agency, and connection.

Student reflections have ranged from personal gratitude over the discovery of the meaning of their names to a deep appreciation of seeing more in their classmates and themselves. The process and results of the W.I.N. are what keep me coming back.

To begin, the students are given the outline and the success criteria as a checklist. They are allotted one period of class time to research the origin and etymology of their name as well as other interesting facts. They write interview questions to ask their parents about why they had chosen their name and what it meant to them. Any additional research and preparation are completed outside of school time. Students were required to present their first and last names, but some even added their middle names or translated their names into another language to add the meaning of that name, too. The students present their projects to the class over 1-2 months because each student selects a date among the teacher-determined options. I usually have 2 students present each day over a 6 week period and not on Friday because I lead a photograph decoding inquiry called Friday Photo each week.

Students always have a lot of positive responses about the W.I.N, and they are the best gauge of the success of any teacher's work. They enjoy the stories about how and why their names were selected, which many had never heard before. A lot of the students learned about the relatives they were named after or whose names and legacies now became theirs. They learned hilarious anecdotes about why they had their name or even the other names they may have had if their other parents had their way. Some parents even wrote to thank me for the opportunity to partake in the interview process for this assignment because they had never thought to discuss their child's name with them as a narrative or because they had a particularly bonding experience with their child through the assignment. More than anything, the students found the project informative and engaging. There were many insightful points that showed a lot of learning from the experience and evidence that we were already building a community.

Through this project, students get to take ownership of an act that, by definition, is something assigned to them by someone external, so this is an empowering approach to seeing your name. It is also a great diagnostic for presentation and research skills.

I build projects. Each of them is just a frame, and what the students bring to them makes each a unique and personal structure. As such, my projects are personalizing as opposed to personalized. Learners can bring to them who and what they are in myriad ways and with a variety of tools. While they all help build skills inside the curriculum, they also help build autonomy, community, and connection. The What's in a Name project also helps students build a sense of identity and cultural literacy. I am grateful that my students always show me *why* the projects need to evolve but not change. These projects are mere outlines, but they invite the whole person to bring themselves into the equation and make them their own. That's what makes it worthwhile to revisit this project time and again. As far as the question of what's in a name, the answer deepens and broadens with every new class.

All BOBs have the same elements: student choice and voice, projects presented to the class community who provide feedback, and the teacher as facilitator. What is unique to this Building Outside the Blocks project is that it invites students to talk about themselves, their family heritage, and the ever-powerful themes of immigration, determination, sacrifice, hope, continuity, loss, and love all through the conduit of a student's name. It can be a proactive way to build an inclusive space where everyone feels visible and valuable.

Whether you love it or hate it, your name has a story, and educators can give students the opportunity to not just investigate that story but to share it with their classes and take their place and their name in the class community. Names can be difficult to pronounce, but kids deserve to feel like they matter enough to hear their names as they are supposed to sound. I have heard teachers mispronounce a student's name every day for an entire school year. Can you imagine going an entire school day without anyone saying your name correctly or, worse, at all? What message does that send?

Names are the first introduction to a person, and they deserve a bit of time for exploration and clarity. The What's in a Name project has students investigating the etymology of their names, the reason why it was chosen for them, its meaning to them and if they chose, any alternative name the student would select. As with all of the BOBs, students don't just fill out the answers to questions. They use the questions outlined in the graphic organizers to guide and personalize their projects and make them into presentations. The W.I.N. is a powerful project to use at the beginning of a school year. Besides being a unique way to introduce the class to each other over the first months of school, it does a lot to build the community from the name up.

What's in a name? Your name is your story. It connects you to the past- to your heritage and traditions, to the language of your people, and to the dreams bestowed upon you with the lifelong gift of a name. It reflects the powerful themes of geography, hope, honor, and loss. The *What's in a Name* project is a high-yielding one, as are most BOBs. It helps develop cultural literacy in a diverse classroom. We learn a lot about family histories and personal identities. The WIN is about belonging to yourself, your family, to your culture and language group, and to the class community. The W.I.N. is an invitation to each student to be part of a community that is being co-constructed, one name at a time.

Student comments:

In Noa Daniel's Grade 8 classroom, this project is under the unit of inquiry titled This is Me which is about identity and memoir. Here are some unedited comments from student reflections on the W.I.N.:

"I feel like a new version of myself because I got to tell everyone the backstory of my name. I loved learning that everyone's name has a different meaning. Everyone is different and comes from backgrounds of different religions from different places, but we all have a lot in common and I'm glad we got to share." -Ethan

"I interviewed my parents and found out that my name was related to the god we believe in. My name comes up in the songs we sing to show gratitude in the Hindu faith. Now that I know more about my name, I wouldn't want to change it. It makes me feel proud to be me and introduce myself." – Riddhi

GRATITUDE
CREATED BY: MANDY FROEHLICH

STANDARD(S)/OBJECTIVE(S)	LEARNING OUTCOME(S)
*Practicing gratitude brings self-awareness by highlighting what we are thankful for in our lives. *It requires us to be intentional about manifesting more of what we are appreciative of into our lives.	A consistent gratitude practice can rewire our brains to have a more positive foundation, and if faced with adversity, our default attitude becomes more centered on being appreciative of what we have.

CONNECTION TO BELONGING

*Based on recent research, gratitude is an intrinsic component of the human experience just like belonging. In fact, grateful people are more helpful and generous, experience higher rates of well-being, and have more prosocial behavior.
*A common misunderstanding is that just the act of writing down what we are thankful for is enough.

OVERARCHING/DRIVING QUESTION	ASSESSMENT
*What is gratitude? *How can we express it?	To really practice gratitude wholly you must also feel the gratitude in your body that your brain has acknowledged.

ACTIVITY

1. Ask participants to write down what they are grateful for according to their five senses. Maybe they are thankful for the smell of the wonderful apple pie that their grandma makes, or the warm bed that they feel when they go to sleep at night. Maybe it was the opportunity to tell their caregiver "Thank you" for their support when they saw them that morning. Depending on their age, they may need help defining an example for each sense.
2. Then, I ask them to choose their favorite thought - the one that brings them the most joy. They need to close their eyes and hold onto it in their mind.
3. Finally, I ask the students to feel that emotion from their toes to their nose by imagining the grateful feeling filling them up like warm sunshine or water - from their toes to their knees, to their hips, and so on.

At the elementary level, this is typically where you see the kids with their eyes closed and smiles on their faces.

This activity is appropriate for any age and is a fantastic way to take the practice of gratitude to fruition. It's not enough just to write it down. The feeling of appreciation and gratitude needs to be felt from the toes to the nose for it really to be impactful.

"I WONDER..." MINDSETS IN THE KITCHEN

SUBMITTED BY: VICTORIA THOMPSON

STANDARD(S)/OBJECTIVE(S)	LEARNING OUTCOME(S)
This is a STEM-based activity that includes math (measurement) and science (processes and wondering/discovery). Language arts and nutrition can also be included.	It is important that students wonder throughout the cooking class, both about the activities at hand and how food relates to who they are.

CONNECTION TO BELONGING

Cooking and eating are activities that bring us together as a community.
Learn about different cultures by learning about their food.
Thinking about our classmates and how we treat them with respect creates an environment for belonging.

OVERARCHING/DRIVING QUESTION	ASSESSMENT
*I wonder..." Students write down what they are wondering about in relation to the cooking activity they will do.	*Note: this was an activity that was NOT graded since it is a community-building activity. However, it can be submitted as a cookbook and assessed for spelling, grammar, description, sentence flow, etc.

ACTIVITY - 60 MINUTES

*Before class begins: For this lesson, students are encouraged to bring a recipe from home, a cultural recipe, or a recipe that they find to be neat from the Internet or the media center (e.g. favorite food, a cool looking food, etc). If students need ideas, they can ask the teacher.

1. Once the students have entered your classroom, have them take out their recipes and have the students do a "gallery walk" around to see the different types of recipes that the students have brought in.
2. Then, students have the opportunity to exchange their recipes with a partner and engage in a 3-2-1 strategy of sharing.
   a. Three things that the listener found interesting about their partner's recipe
   b. Two things they learned about their partner while listening to them describe their recipe
   c. One "wondering" or one thing that they'd like to learn more about after hearing about the recipe
3. Students have the opportunity to share one thing that they learned from their partner.

4. Now, for the fun part: with the recipes that we had brought into class, the culmination of the class was the announcement of a class cookbook! To do this, explain that the class is going to be making a cookbook with the recipes that were brought in. Each student was to create a recipe card with the following:
- The title of their recipe
- The ingredients needed for the recipe
- The steps to complete the recipe
- A picture of the completed recipe
- A description of their recipe; specifically, they explained why they chose that particular dish, what that dish means to them, described a special time they ate it or the first time that they had it, and anything else they thought readers should know about it. They checked for language errors and that the recipes followed the correct format and were clear to understand.

5. Once all students are complete with the recipe cards, the teacher will put them into a book and it will become part of the class library.

6. Then, at the end of the course, we had a party during one of our class periods where we made the food items (or brought in the food items if they were more elaborate) and invited students from other classes, faculty members, and even family members to come in and celebrate our journey to belonging in the STEM cooking classroom and the various different types of cultures and foods that help make our class unique.

LESSONS AND ACTIVITIES FOR PERSONAL BELONGING

WHAT IS PERSONAL BELONGING?

Empathetic educators know who their students are, and this helps build and strengthen their relationships and personalize interactions. They model their interactions with others for their students. For instance, while students are engaged in group work, a teacher can carefully observe and tell a student, "I can see that you're showing respect to your team members by listening to what they're saying." Empathy, compassion, inclusion, equity, and social justice are all part of instilling a sense of personal belonging in your classroom. Our students are diverse in so many ways and we need to be mindful of that when we're planning and facilitating learning. Each and every learner should have the chance to excel in your classroom. This chapter, which aligns with Chapter 4 in *Journey to Belonging*, focuses on some ways you can do that.

"MY TOWN"

CREATED BY: DR. ILENE WINOKUR

STANDARD(S)/OBJECTIVE(S)	LEARNING OUTCOME(S)
Standards related to social studies and civics can be applied to this activity. It can also become an extended project.	Students will explore and discover the necessary components that make up a community that is inclusive, accepting of all, and ensures each person feels a sense of belonging.

CONNECTION TO BELONGING

When we connect with people in our community, we feel a sense of belonging.
There are certain components necessary for people to feel a sense of belonging within a community.
This project explores the concept of inclusive and equitable community spaces.

OVERARCHING/DRIVING QUESTION	ASSESSMENT
*What is a community and how do we cultivate a sense of belonging and caring for each other?	Create a rubric that highlights the outcomes and expectations of the project. They can include specific skills like inquiry and problem-solving and/or creativity, depending on the subject area and grade level.

ACTIVITY

1. Students are shown or can share different models of communities including schools, residential areas, urban, or rural areas.
2. The teacher facilitates discussion about what makes up a community.
3. Students work in groups or individually to design a community space based on the principles of an inclusive and accepting community.

Here is a video for high school students that can be used to prompt discussion and help students with ideas for the community they will build.

https://journeys2belonging.com/32B3XFP

You can prompt their thinking by showing photos of various communities around the world. Be sure to include communities that represent where your students are from in addition to others. Be sensitive to students who are newcomers or immigrants and have suffered trauma as a result of leaving home.

Here is the link to the TIME Kids website that has a number of articles and ideas about Community:

https://journeys2belonging.com/33TOLUQ

5 - 20 - 3

CREATED BY: TAN HUYNH

STANDARD(S)/OBJECTIVE(S)

5 - 20 - 3 is a quick student–driven presentation to share a holiday from their culture.

LEARNING OUTCOME(S)

Students create a presentation at home to share with the class on the day of the holiday.

CONNECTION TO BELONGING

This strategy allows students to be seen and recognized even if they are not from the most dominant culture. It's a quick way to share students' culture with classmates and to make it interactive.

OVERARCHING/DRIVING QUESTION

*What is the significance of this holiday?
*What does this holiday mean to you?

ASSESSMENT

Create a rubric to assess presentation skills including how well they are able to respond to questions.
Have students assess themselves based on pre-set deadlines and whether they met them on time.

ACTIVITY

The activity's structure is:
5 photos
20 seconds to talk about each photo
3 questions from students after the presentation

CREATING A SENSE OF COMMUNITY AND BELONGING

CREATED BY: JANIQUE CASELEY

STANDARD(S)/OBJECTIVE(S)

Strengthen a sense of belonging and classroom community using indigenous teachings about building character and finding balance to become a strong citizen and community member.

LEARNING OUTCOME(S)

Students take ownership over their own actions and are more mindful of being respectful, truthful, humble, loving, and courageous. After all, they have a visual that they created together every day to remind them!

CONNECTION TO BELONGING

Creating these norms together in this way has nurtured a sense of community that I had not experienced before, and I had always involved students in creating their classroom "rules".

OVERARCHING/DRIVING QUESTION

*What is a community and what is each individual's role within it?

ASSESSMENT

Throughout the year, ask students to self-assess based on the classroom norms and definitions they created after reading the story.

ACTIVITY

Background:

A sense of community and a sense of belonging are two synonymous ideas. One cannot exist without the other. The opportunity to start creating a sense of community presents itself on the first day of school and certainly builds within those first few weeks. It is created in the way we greet our students, welcome them to our classroom community, and develop a set of norms in how we want to work and treat each other throughout our year together.

One way to create a set of expectations for every member of a classroom community is with the use of the book *The Lost Teachings* (*Panuijkatasikl Kina'masuti'l*) by Michael James Isaac. This book is an aboriginal story of seven sacred teachings that were passed down from generation to generation. It is the story of striving for balance, harmony, and peace while dealing with envy and greed at the same time, and how sometimes we lose our way. As one journeys through the story with Eagle, one hears about seven important characteristics that help build strong character, as well as how envy and greed present themselves sometimes in life. It is a beautiful story of how to find a balance to become a strong citizen and community member.

In our classroom community, within the first week of school, we begin our conversations about our class norms, how we would like to be treated, and how we should treat others. This lesson usually takes two one-hour classes to complete, sometimes three, depending on the conversations. The conversations for the second part of the lesson can be quite rich with ideas, and listening to all of the voices may take time, but it is worth it!

Preparations:
You will need to have each of the seven teaching words on pieces of paper: Honesty, Wisdom, Respect, Love, Humility, Courage, and Truth. On the eighth piece of paper, the words "Beware of Envy and Greed" should be printed. Also have on paper the seven definitions, which are as follows:

- Never lie, cheat, or steal.
- Be proud of yourself and be kind to everyone, even those who are different from you. Also, be kind to the environment.
- Care for those who are not as strong or as fortunate as you, without asking or expecting anything in return.
- No matter how much you know, you should never think you're better than anyone else. Everyone has something to teach you if you let them.
- Know the difference between right and wrong and take responsibility for your actions.
- Consider the interest of others before your own and speak up for what is right.
- Learn from your mistakes. It is better to live with the truth than to live with a lie. If you stand with those who believe in truth and speak from the heart, the truth will be yours.

Part One:

1. Hang each of the seven words around your classroom so they are visible to everyone.
2. Read each word aloud so everyone hears them.
3. Take one definition at a time, read it aloud, then ask the class which word they think the definition belongs to. When they come to a consensus, hang the definition next to the word.
4. As more definitions are read, sometimes the class will change their mind about a previously placed definition. Give the opportunity for those conversations to happen and allow them to change where the definitions are placed if they all agree.
5. Once all seven definitions are hung next to the words, also hang up the paper that says, "Beware of Envy and Greed". Discuss what both of those words mean so there is a common understanding of each word.
6. Next is to read the story. As the story is being read, when each word and definition is revealed, ask your students to check that the definition matches the word correctly on the wall. If it doesn't, ask a student to locate the matching definition for the word and change the papers on the wall.
7. At the end of the story, once each word has been matched with the definition given by Eagle, have a discussion about whether anything surprised them or stands out to them which is a great way to end this part of the lesson.

Part Two: This part may take a couple of classes, depending on the time that you have each day. It is a very valuable part and it is important to take the time to have the conversations that will arise. Still, with the words and definitions on the walls, go through each word one at a time. Ask the students how they would define each word for creating a safe and supportive classroom community. Together, come up with a definition for each word that describes how everyone in the community should act to establish a learning environment that is supportive of everyone. Record the definition for everyone to see and read.

Part Three: Once all of the classroom definitions have been established for the seven words, further activity is to ask the students in groups to collaborate and create an art piece to illustrate one of the words and the respective definition. It amazes me how, independently, most groups choose to create an art piece with the focal point being one of the animals from the story. However, there have been other ways students have chosen to illustrate the teachings as well. Students enjoy being creative and collaborating with each other, and it is a great opportunity for them to choose how they want to represent the classroom norms.

After the art pieces have been finished, we hang the words, definitions, and artworks in the classroom. We will read each definition every day for the first month or two, and then we reference them throughout the year at times when we are noticing an act demonstrating one of the words or to remind someone gently of our classroom norms.

Creating these norms together in this way has nurtured a sense of community that I had not experienced before, and I had always involved students in creating their classroom "rules". Students take ownership over their own actions now and are more mindful of being respectful, truthful, humble, loving, and courageous. After all, they have a visual that they created together every day to remind them!

OUR FAMILY QUILT

CREATED BY: JUSTIN GARCIA

STANDARD(S)/OBJECTIVE(S)

Content objective: I can illustrate and describe my family with a partner.
Language objective: I can orally use "I have a/an _____" using target vocabulary related to family members to describe my family with a partner.

LEARNING OUTCOME(S)

Students learn that there are many ways to look at what makes up a family.

Vocabulary: family, sibling, community, quilt, family words (brother, sister, aunt, uncle, etc. depending on your teaching context)

CONNECTION TO BELONGING

Our relationship with our family is an important part of our identity and belonging. It's important to understand the different ways we can talk about and view our families.

OVERARCHING/DRIVING QUESTION

*What is a family?
*Who is in your family?
*What do families do?

ASSESSMENT

Display the vocabulary in front of the class and the sentence stem, "I have a/an _____."
For example, "I have a husband named Barrak."
You can extend these sentence stems to be as simple or complex as you like based on the context of your class.

Model examples of sharing the teacher square with a partner. Using the sentence stems and vocabulary, ask for volunteers to model sharing their squares with a partner in front of the class. Students can then share with their peers independently or, if they're uncomfortable sharing, they can write their responses or share with the teacher.

Before teaching:
The purpose of this lesson is to learn about different family structures and dynamics. Be prepared for students to have internalized a family as being a "mom and dad". If you know students in your class have different family structures that they may be sensitive to discussing with the class, have a talk with them before this lesson to get a temperature check to avoid them being singled out or feeling uncomfortable. For example, one student in my class has two moms and had been bullied the previous year. I pulled her aside ahead of time and asked her what would help her feel more comfortable participating in this lesson. She expressed her concern about being singled out, so I took precautions to make sure other students would respect her boundaries.**

Grade levels: Early primary, but can be adapted for older grades.
Time: 45-60 minutes
Materials: 5x5 paper/fabric squares (I used paper. Squares can be any size), pre-made teacher example, coloring tools, anchor text(s)*

Pre-read the texts to find appropriate stopping points for discussion ahead of time.

Anticipatory set: Activate background knowledge by using the following questions or adapting them to fit your context:

"What is a family?" "Who is in your family?" "What do families do?"

Objective: Share the content and language objective with the class. (see above)
Direct instruction: Describe how families can be different in many ways. Some families have two parents, some have one parent, some have no parent, and some are "chosen families". Families can have parents of a variety of genders: men, women, nonbinary people, etc. Students will likely ask what these terms mean; provide them with a brief, factual definition and continue with the lesson.

Introduce the chosen anchor text. Ask what students notice and wonder about the cover. Ask what families they will find in the story.

**This is the point where I explained to the students the importance of respecting others' privacy and that singling people out can be uncomfortable.
Read through the story and encourage dialogue throughout the reading. You can ask some or all of the following questions:

How are these families similar/different from yours?
How do these families support each other?
How do these families show love for one another?
What if someone made fun of your family for being different? How would you feel? What would you do?
What would you do if you *saw or heard* someone making fun of someone else's family?

After the reading, reflect on what everyone saw and learned from the story. This is a good point to introduce family vocabulary words tailored to your teaching context. I like to create cards with pictures and vocabulary in English and other languages that reflect my classroom.

Next, introduce the activity. Share that the class will be making a class "quilt" with pictures of our families. Show pictures of a quilt with different types of squares and designs if needed. Share the pre-prepared teacher square with a drawing of the teacher's family and labels with names.

Independent Practice: Students take 25–30 minutes (or as long as they need) to illustrate their own family quilt. Play some zen music and let them create.

Additional information:

*The anchor texts this lesson uses are texts about families, and they are inclusive to diverse families. Here are some recommended texts:

A Family is a Family is a Family by Sara O'Leary and Qin Leng
And Tango Makes Three by Justin Richardson, Peter Parnell, and Henry Cole
Families by Shelley Rotner and Sheila M. Kelly
Our Class is a Family by Shannon Olsen and Sandie Sonke
Ohana Means Family by Ilima Loomis and Kenard Pak

MY CLASSROOM FAMILY

CREATED BY: MELISA HAYES

STANDARD(S)/OBJECTIVE(S)	LEARNING OUTCOME(S)
Depending on grade level, various language arts or social studies standards can be applied.	Students will participate in a variety of activities that instill a sense of personal belonging and relationships in their classroom.

CONNECTION TO BELONGING

Promoting community enables belonging and empowers students. Including their families increases their sense of belonging.

OVERARCHING/DRIVING QUESTION	ASSESSMENT
*What is a class family? *How do we treat each other so each of us feels included?	An assessment can be created but this activity isn't intended to be assessed.

ACTIVITY

Background:

My philosophy and why I teach are simple. It's all about my family! No, this isn't my immediate family but my classroom family. Yep, I call my kids "family". From the moment they introduce themselves on the Flip (formerly Flipgrid) app before school starts until they graduate high school, they are my kids! It's not all about academics but the sense of belonging my family feels within our classroom. It's vital that each of my kids feels empowered, important, and special! They need to drive the bus in their education and have a voice in every task that's completed. It's not about me; it's about them!

One activity I do with my 2nd-grade family is to have them create what our promise should state. I break them into groups with chart paper and they share in a group what they want our family promise to be. We put all the papers together for a gallery walk. Finally, we create the promise based on all the ideas, and the kids as well as I sign our promise and add a drawing of ourselves. This is a constant reminder of how we want our family to look, feel, and act.

1. My kids also create a playlist of songs for them to hear every morning as they do soft starts. This is a time when each of my kids can bond, laugh, talk, explore, play, and more. My family can read a book, or play a game. Code, draw, work a puzzle, explore AR/VR, and more. This time is so critical for my family to get to know each other, enjoy each other's company, cheer each other up, or explore something new.
2. We love dance parties and had them daily on Zoom this year! It's important to have fun with your kids! This improves both your and your kids' mental health!
3. Finally my kids love participating in our kindness project.

We do this activity each year. It occurs around the last couple of months of school when my kids know each other best. Each child sits in the hot seat with their back to the chalkboard and a small group is called to come up and writes positive messages about that child in the hot seat. I continue calling each group until every child has come up to share something positive about the kiddo in the hot seat. Once every child has written their message, I count back from 3 and then say, turn around. The look on the child's face when they see the messages and then read them is priceless. It's an emotional activity that's so powerful! I can't say enough about how much each child feels worthy, important, and belongs!

Whatever activity or idea you choose, remember to establish your family! Make time for them to laugh every day! Share the celebrations, struggles, and accomplishments. Family is everything and your kids are only in that grade once. Make it memorable:)
Here's a video of my class Kindness project from a few years ago.

https://journeys2belonging.com/3AB8Afr

AN INVITATION TO BRAVE SPACE

CREATED BY: ROLA TBSHIRANI

STANDARD(S)/OBJECTIVE(S)

Students learn to use a set of thinking tools to build their self-awareness and understanding of different perspectives.

LEARNING OUTCOME(S)

Students will learn to use thinking tools to build self-awareness and perspective-taking.

CONNECTION TO BELONGING

*How are we building a community of brave space where students' voices are valued?
We need to give opportunities for students to share perspectives and build relationships for a brave and safe classroom culture that leads to a sense of belonging.

*Skills like self-awareness, perspective-taking, and understanding are all part of self-belonging.

OVERARCHING/DRIVING QUESTION

*What is Brave Space?
*How can we, as individuals, contribute to creating a Brave Space?

ASSESSMENT

Ask students to put their thoughts/reflections in a journal to track their growing self-awareness (draw, write, sketch, record audio or video).

ACTIVITY

Project Zero thinking tools are great tools to implement with students for building relationships.

Project Zero Thinking Routines
The steps and links are included on this document:

https://journeys2belonging.com/3TNu168

What can I do in my inner circle (of friends, family, the people I know)?

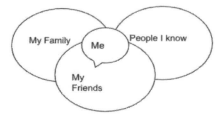

5- The 3 Whys

> # Why might this question/topic matter to me?

6- How are we making meaning and what speaks to students?

7- The Ladder of Inference

Intense discussions and jumping to conclusions could affect community building. We can jump to conclusions that can be explained by a mental model, the Ladder of Inference. The Ladder of Inference can be used as a tool and a communication tool to improve students' and teachers' decision-making. A video Explaining the Ladder of Inference is also one of the thinking tools. The link is on the Google doc mentioned above.

Below is the image I use on the Jamboard that students could apply the Ladder of Inference for any data collection about their self-awareness, their social-emotional learning, videos, characters from books, and images.

Prompts to make our thinking explicit

Conclusion
- I conclude.../ My model is...
- What do I believe to be true about this situation?

Interpret Data
- I think... I assume... This means...
- This is significant because...
- What does this data mean to me?
- What do I assume to be true about this data?

Data and Select Data
- I see...
- To what extent is my data pool complete?
- What data is missing?
- What prior knowledge am I including?
- What data do I consider to be most significant?
- What other data should I be paying attention to?
- Why am I choosing this data?

INCLUSIVE PRACTICES FOR LANGUAGE LEARNERS

Imagine that you traveled to a country where the people don't speak English. How would you communicate with others about your basic needs like a place to stay, your meals, and what parts of the city are safe? Would you panic or feel scared? What would you need to feel safe? How could others who speak the local language help and support you to make you feel safe? This is how language learners often feel in your classroom. English learners in Kuwait's private schools often lack confidence in their ability to communicate in English, and immigrants around the world face similar obstacles.

Newcomer students may also be coming from a traumatic situation if they're a newcomer or recently resettled. Your role as a teacher in making sure they feel safe is vital if they're going to succeed in your classroom. If they've been uprooted from their homes due to war or a natural disaster, they lack a sense of belonging because they were forced to leave their homes. They may have gaps in their education due to displacement or are unfamiliar with the local language. We know that all students need to feel a sense of belonging at school and "[w]hile a sense of belonging is necessary for all students to succeed in school, students from immigrant and refugee backgrounds are particularly affected." What do we mean by belonging? Naashia Mohamed explains,

> Students' sense of belonging refers to the feelings of being accepted by teachers, peers, and any other individuals at school, and feeling like they are part of the school community. When students feel that they are a part of a school community, they are more likely to perform better academically and are more motivated to learn. Studies also show that the feelings of security, identity, and community associated with a sense of belonging affect students' psychological well-being and social development.[1]

It's important to establish a safe environment that begins with trust and respectful relationships from the first day of class. All students need to believe they are treated fairly, so if accommodations are made for some students, including language learners, their peers need to be aware of the reasons you are scaffolding their lessons. In addition, there are several steps you can take to ensure all of your students feel a sense of belonging like greeting them as they enter your physical or virtual classroom each day. Another step is making sure you pronounce their names correctly. Sometimes students who are new will be shy about correcting their teacher so explain that it's important to you. After all, it's part of their identity.

Another way to increase your students' sense of belonging is by creating an environment of caring, collaboration, respect, empathy, and compassion among your students. Modeling this whether you're inside your classroom or with your students or colleagues will go a long way to showing your students the way. We need to make sure our students don't feel like the *others*. In an article for the Haas Institute for a Fair and Inclusive Society (Berkeley), john a. powell and Stephen Menendian (2016) define "othering" as a set of dynamics, processes, and structures that engender marginality and persistent inequality across any of the full range of human differences based on group identities. Dimensions of othering include but are not limited to, religion, sex, race, ethnicity, socioeconomic status (class), disability, sexual orientation, and skin tone (p. 14).

You might be saying to yourself, 'How do I handle differentiated lessons or accommodations for my students? Won't that make them feel different and othered? Truthfully, it won't if you handle it correctly. If your students know you have their best interests at heart because you've shown them you care about how they're progressing in your class, they won't focus on how you're delivering the lesson. Also, they will champion your efforts to ensure their success if you explain to them, from the beginning of the year, that each student has different needs, strengths, and areas that need improvement. Your job is to help them reach the stated outcomes by supporting their efforts, celebrating their successes, and giving them focused feedback to support their progress.

After I became elementary principal, I continued to read, research, and present new teaching strategies to the teachers on my team. At one point, I read about adding language objectives to lesson plans alongside content objectives. There is a great need for teachers to include both in order to remain focused on language acquisition for language learners and content for all your learners. Using language objectives in your planning helps you focus on the needs of your language learners and is useful for students who have language-related disabilities or need extra support to learn vocabulary for comprehension. It's also a more inclusive way to teach.

There are some terrific resources for setting up language objectives. Sites like WIDA[2] and Colorin' Colorado[3] can help you get started with language objectives in your planning. Structured Instruction Observation Protocol (SIOP)[4] is another research-based and useful tool for planning your lessons. You will find videos and descriptions of the eight elements of SIOP in my Wakelet collection of resources for ELL instruction.[5] (See the QR code below for the link.)

Teaching ELLs in the Content Areas and ELA (Wakelet collection)

One of the most important strategies to remember when planning lessons for language learners is scaffolding. Just like a building needs a scaffold until its frame is solid, students need supports or scaffolds to help them build basic language skills and then, eventually, the scaffolds can be taken away once they are confident and have achieved some mastery of outcomes. According to Rebecca Alber (2011)[6],

> Scaffolding is breaking up the learning into chunks and providing a tool, or structure, with each chunk. When scaffolding reading, for example, you might preview the text and discuss key vocabulary, or chunk the text and then read and discuss as you go.

Alber lists six general scaffolding strategies including the teacher modeling for students using think-alouds, retrieving prior knowledge, and pre-teaching key or content vocabulary which is supported by language objectives. When students who are struggling to understand directions and key content objectives are supported with a variety of scaffolds, their affective filter (Krashen, 1982)[7] is reduced and they are more motivated and less fearful of trying out their new language skills. The affective filter is commonly described as "an imaginary wall that rises in the mind and prevents input, thus blocking cognition," and Valentina Gonzalez continues in her blog post, "Creating classroom environments that act intentionally to lower the affective filter will increase language development. The lower the filter, the more input is allowed to pass through. Students who are highly motivated, feel confident, and feel safe are more open to input."[8]

What is the Affective Filter and Why is it Important (Seidliz Education)

Lowering the affective filter reduces the fear of failing and ensures a sense of safety. As I noted in Chapter 2 of *Journey to Belonging*, according to Polyvagal Theory (Porges, 2004)[9] signals from the autonomic nervous system trigger immediate reactions of fight, flight, or shut down when it feels any type of threat or lack of safety. The brain is connected to the major organs of our body through the vagus nerve. Polyvagal Theory helps us understand the connection between our emotions, responses to different situations, and our need for co-regulation through connection with others. In order to co-regulate, we must first be able to self-regulate. In order to self-regulate, students need the right conditions and support from their teachers. It's important to model and support students as they navigate building personal strategies and coping skills for self-regulation since some students are not ready or able to do that. Specific learning strategies include giving focused and constructive feedback after students complete a task, instilling a growth mindset and mindfulness, helping students set up a way to track their progress, and having them look at their work with a more problem-solving lens that enables them to find their mistakes and what they can do to overcome them in the future. For example, after taking a test, students can focus on incorrect answers to figure out what caused them to get it wrong.[10] Teachers can guide them through this process by talking through steps they can take to analyze their answers. Learning to self-regulate helps all learners, especially language learners or those who need more support.

Poly...What? An Intro to Polyvagal Theory (Rachel Sellers)

Principles and Practice in Second Language Instruction
(Stephen Krashen)

The Importance of Self-Regulation for Learning (The Education
Hub)

Students who are learning a new language often lack the confidence to use the language and may also be afraid of being noticed as different by classmates. As the brain begins to signal a lack of safety, it forms a barrier to learning. Our instruction must include ways to reduce anxiety and stress and increase a sense of safety by ensuring students have a voice and choice whenever possible and are made to feel they are the center of the learning. We should use an asset-based approach that includes the belief that all students can learn but some may take longer. When teachers communicate expectations, we need to do it in a way that lowers the affective filter and shows that our students' success is important to us and we are going to facilitate and support them to reach mastery of the skills.

*From blog post by Valentina Gonzalez[11]

BACKPACK OF EXPERIENCES
Created by: Dr. Denise Furlong

Objective/Outcome:	Connection to Belonging:
Fostering a sense of belonging and connection with newcomer students	Making connections with our newcomers is vital for them to thrive in our classroom.

Belonging... How does one foster a sense of belonging for students who are new to the country? What they bring with them in their **"backpack of experiences"** is so diverse and unique to each child. They may speak unfamiliar languages, come from countries that are distant geographically or culturally, and have life experiences outside the realm of our understanding. How can we leverage what we know about them to invite them to share in our collective journey together?

The first thing we do to make these connections with our new students is to try to **see things from their perspective** to really understand what their experience might be like. I often think of a Newcomer's first days in school like a Funhouse at the carnival or boardwalk. Things may seem not as they appear, there are crazy changes around every corner, and there is a feeling of unease and possible anxiety about what is to come. These are the conversations we have in class before we even meet our Newcomers. Putting oneself in another's shoes is a powerful way to inspire **empathy** among the peers of our Newcomers.

It's crucial that the teacher model behavior that is inviting and receptive for the arrival of our Newcomers. **"We are going to have a new member join our class family and I am so excited for us all to meet them and learn from them!"** Students certainly feel when the teacher is stressed or anxious about meeting the needs of the new students, and it's important to make it clear that this is something positive. Also, students must know that no matter what amount of language they know or what schooling they have had, there are many things that they can learn from our Newcomers.

Once our Newcomer is in class with us, we have a variety of ways to help foster their sense of belonging as a vital member of our group. We may make **welcome posters** attempting to use their home language to show them how happy we are that they are joining us. Taking the time as a teacher to meet them, smile, and attempt a greeting in the student's home language is something that will help them feel belonging. Peer buddies are great and should include both students who speak our Newcomer's home language (if possible) and students who do not. The more students who are creating relationships with our Newcomer, the better; these students all become **stakeholders** in the new student's success.

As our Newcomer settles into our class family, there are still ways that we can foster a sense of belonging for everyone.

- Students can learn how to greet people in all of the languages of the class family. We can also practice saying **"Bless you!"** and other key phrases. There is a lot of laughter and interaction during these exchanges because the learning is done in an active and fun way.

- Classroom and hallway **decorations** should include the languages and cultures of the classroom family.

- Allow our Newcomer to write their own narrative and create their own identity. Instead of asking specifically for them to detail their trip or talk about prior schooling or home country, ask them to write or draw something they choose to share with you or the class family. Giving them a voice about what they elect to share with their new class empowers them to be in charge of **the new chapter of their story**.

- Treat our Newcomer as an **expert** in their language and culture and integrate things about their country into lessons or quick transitions if possible. Or if they appear to be uncomfortable with the spotlight, simply sharing fun facts every morning about the cultures in the class may be appropriate.

- Ensure that our Newcomer's language and culture are well represented in **literature** in the classroom and in **curricula**. This may not happen overnight, but engaging the school media specialist is a great way to facilitate this.

- The **silent period** is real! When students are still in the phase of "taking it all in" rather than speaking and interacting with classmates and teachers, they are still learning, engaging, and growing.

- When providing critical information for our Newcomers, doing so in the home language is kind and inclusive. With all of the technological tools at our fingertips, we may not be 100% accurate in our attempts, but we can certainly use **communication in the home language** to foster a sense of belonging.

Remember that what the teacher does to be **inclusive** for every member of the "class family" is what the students internalize and take with them from your class forward. These children (including our Newcomers!) are current and future leaders and learn from your example. Focus on belonging for everyone and interact with each student from an **asset-based perspective**. ALL of your students will thank you for it.

BELONGING AND PROJECT-BASED LEARNING (PBL)

My experience teaching English in Kuwait at the grade 3 level and pre-college intensive courses spans 25 years. Within that time, I have tried numerous methods to support my students' English language acquisition while overcoming their lack of confidence and negative self-talk (lack of self-belonging) about learning the language. My action research shows a direct link between the achievement of language and content objectives through project-based learning (PBL). The best resource for PBL is the Buck Institute for Education: PBL Works

Students work on a project over an extended period of time – from a week up to a semester – that engages them in solving a real-world problem or answering a complex question. They demonstrate their knowledge and skills by creating a public product or presentation for a real audience.

As a result, students develop deep content knowledge as well as critical thinking, collaboration, creativity, and communication skills. Project-Based Learning unleashes contagious, creative energy among students and teachers.

PBL is authentic learning that is meaningful to students. They make connections to their interests, and background knowledge, and learn the language throughout the process. Writing, reading, listening, and speaking are all necessary components of the projects. They are making meaning and connections to the learning because it's meaningful to them.

According to PBL Works, English Language Learners are one of the groups that tend to be looked over when thinking about who is "ready" to do PBL. But all students are ready if armed with appropriate scaffolding by their teacher. In fact, if we look at learning in terms of growth, EL students are likely to show huge success due to how immersive PBL is in communication skills and critical thinking.

Projects can be tailored to any and all subjects. When using this method with language learners, scaffolding is a must. Planning by the teacher must be intentional and well-thought-out. PBL mentions several scaffolding strategies for successful PBL planning with language learners. I have summarized them here:

- Research must be accessible and students shouldn't be left on their own to search. They should be guided to look for podcasts, leveled books, short articles, etc. that can be chunked into smaller bits. Model the search and

research process the first time they're assigned a
project.

- Provide background vocabulary of keywords to
  support them. Building schema around the topic gives
  students valuable context before beginning the project.
  This supports their confidence and efficacy when they
  encounter words or phrases they're unfamiliar with.
  Help them make connections to their prior knowledge.

- Depending on the student's level of language fluency,
  provide visuals for instructions such as pictures, gifs, or
  icons. Videos using Screencastify to record your
  instructions give the student a way to view them
  multiple times or stop at certain points.

- Set the stage from the beginning of the year by teaching
  collaboration to all of your students. Don't assume they
  know how to work together. This is where empathy,
  sharing of ideas, and resources through teamwork
  support their feeling of personal belonging.
  Collaboration creates respect for others and helps them
  embrace differences.

- Teachers should be actively involved in interacting
  with students as they work in groups. Asking tiered
  questions that guide students towards the next short-
  term goal is essential. Keep anecdotal notes of student
  progress and let them know you value what they're
  doing.

- Post project progress timelines, keywords, and related
  resources on a bulletin board and keep adding to it for
  the duration of the project. This will provide ongoing

support to students who might not work as quickly as others.

You may be wondering how PBL Works recommends assessing students working on projects. They have created a set of research-based rubrics with four main areas: Critical Thinking, Collaboration, Self-Directed Learning, and Complex Communication. The rubrics act as a guide for giving focused feedback to students about their progress in each area from Beginning, Emerging, Developing, to Demonstrating. When using these rubrics, they recommend teachers modify them based on local context.

Learning a new language in an academic environment is daunting, so creating ways to integrate feelings of belonging (validation, acceptance, feeling valued, having agency) while conquering the language and content objectives will go a long way toward successful achievement of those goals. Project-based learning that is planned for and implemented well can help students accomplish it all.

The use of scaffolds, language objectives, and project-based learning are some of the inclusive strategies that will lower the affective filter of students who need more time learning the target language. They will be more motivated to learn and less likely to worry about failing if they try to use it. Their self-efficacy in the target language will increase and they will achieve skill mastery faster.

USING KAHOOT! TO DEVELOP A SENSE OF BELONGING

CREATED BY: DR. CAROL SALVA

STANDARD(S)/OBJECTIVE(S)

The goal is to have students share about themselves, appreciate the assets of their classmates, and think critically. The ultimate goal is to use this activity with content, capitalizing on the sense of competence and relationships that have been established.

LEARNING OUTCOME(S)

Students increase their inter- and intra-personal skills.

CONNECTION TO BELONGING

Self-awareness and appreciation for our strengths, knowing our interests, and our ability to share them with others supports our personal growth and path to self-belonging.

OVERARCHING/DRIVING QUESTION

Who am I?

ASSESSMENT

Kahoot! is an assessment tool.

https://journeys2belonging.com/3RGaK4M.

ACTIVITY

Background:

I work with learners who are new to English, so opportunities to practice language and speak in authentic ways are critical parts of my lesson planning. Speaking about our content is going to help all students internalize what we want them to learn (Zwiers, 2011). This activity offers students an opportunity to analyze and think critically about how to structure a quiz. Students will be required to create questions and answers that include distractors. These are important skills as today's learners are being evaluated on higher-order cognitive skills such as interpreting, synthesizing, communicating, and problem-solving. (Davidson, 2011).

STEPS:

As the teacher, create a Kahoot (an online quiz) about yourself. Include questions about your heritage, hobbies, and personal life. This is an opportunity to show students that you value culture and want them to get to know you. This is great at the beginning of the year but can be done at any time.

Play Kahoot and use the opportunity to echo read. My students are engaged when we play Kahoot!. I take this opportunity to echo-read each question before we move to the next question. Reading aloud in unison (choral reading and echo reading) has been shown to support fluency (Morra & Tracey, 2006) and it offers a low-stress way to practice pronunciation.

Have students give you one trivia question about themselves so you can create one or more quizzes about the class. Even students with low levels of literacy can provide a question by using paper templates or online forms.

Consider repeating this activity with other content. Students can create these assessments about
Classroom norms
Holiday traditions
Hobbies
Any content area of learning.

As we review content, it is important to keep in mind that students can create our reviews. We can give students the correct answer and ask them to come up with distractors. They can do this in teams and it boosts cognitive thinking to a much higher level.

Consider sharing your class Selfie Kahoots with the world. This video (https://journeys2belonging.com/3KWvtPJ)
offers an example of the positive outcomes we have enjoyed. It includes a connection we made with Emily Francis' class. They include self-esteem boost, authentic writing opportunities, global learning, cultural diversity appreciation, and more...

Give it a try!
More on ways to use Kahoot with English Learners.

https://journeys2belonging.com/3BgJ9Sr

More information:
Morra, J. & Tracey, D. H. (2006). The impact of multiple fluency interventions on a single subject. *Reading Horizons: A Journal of Literacy and Language Arts, 47*(2), 175-199.
Zwiers, J., & Crawford, M. (2011). *Academic conversations: Classroom talk that fosters critical thinking and content understandings.* Stenhouse Publishers.

LESSONS AND ACTIVITIES FOR PROFESSIONAL BELONGING

WHAT IS PROFESSIONAL BELONGING?

Creating a sense of belonging at school or in the workplace takes mindfulness and deliberate effort. For employees to feel a sense of belonging, they must believe the organization cares about them, respects them, and values them. In a school setting, administrators, teachers, and staff must feel seen and heard which means they are part of the team that makes decisions whenever possible and they can voice concerns without fear of negative consequences. An additional resource is this article in *Edutopia* about professional learning and belonging.[1] In Chapter 5 of *Journey to Belonging*, I retell stories of my professional belonging and how much it is connected to my professional learning communities, online and offline. We spend a lot of time at work and our mental health and attitude toward what we do depend on how we feel when we walk in the door of the building or get online for a meeting. This chapter is all about ways that YOU can feel a sense of belonging and well-being at and about work.

Professional Learning and Belonging (Edutopia)

SELF-CARE TIPS FOR BUSY EDUCATORS

Created by: Dr. Ilene Winokur

Objective/Outcome:	Connection to Belonging:
Self-care tips for busy educators	If we aren't taking care of our well-being, we will be unable to take care of others, including our students. Self-care means we value ourselves.

Below are some suggestions for self-care and mindfulness to keep yourself balanced and centered.

PROACTIVE WAYS TO TAKE CARE OF YOURSELF:

1. Remind yourself every morning what is within your control.

For example, if you are teaching remotely and some of your students aren't signing on regularly or you haven't heard from a student, consider what you can do to try and contact them. Perhaps a phone call to the student's parents, or checking in with the appropriate person at your school (counselor, team lead, principal) will get them to "attend." If you've tried that and it didn't work then think of other ways to communicate what the student is missing (including the engaging activities you've planned), or use the LMS or apps like Seesaw, Flipgrid, Wakelet, Buncee to entice them.

If you've reflected on your efforts and nothing seems to

be working, do what's in your control. Concentrate on teaching the students who are showing up.

2. Surround yourself with colleagues who are proactive, problem-solvers, and hopeful.

When we have negativity and complaining around us, it's hard to resist getting into that mode of thinking. So it's important to express to others that you need those around you to be centered and focused on the tasks at hand and not worry about what the world could be if it was perfect.

3. Be a good listener to others and make sure it's mutual.

A good listener hears and internalizes what the other person is saying and validates what they've heard by giving feedback that is compassionate and says, "I hear you and I understand what you're saying."

4. Recall what you're grateful for.

List a few things you appreciate and focus on how it makes your life better or happier. One idea is to create a gratitude jar for small slips of paper that you can write down what you're grateful for. Then on the days you can't think of anything or are feeling down, you can take a few out and read them and remember.

5. Show someone kindness.

You can show kindness in many ways like a smile or a kind word.

6. Reach out to others and ask how they're doing.

Some people don't reach out when they need a helping hand or someone to just listen to them share their thoughts or worries. Be the person who asks how they're doing. Send them a message or call on the phone.

These are just a few ways to practice self-care that don't take a lot of time but can become habits that boost you when you're feeling stressed or anxious. It's been hard for me too, although I'm not working full time. I am safe and well, but I'm missing my family. I haven't seen my daughter since last November and my eldest son for even longer. My 96-year-old mother wonders when/if she will see me again…

This is my self-care routine:

When I wake up every morning, I remind myself what day it is (without a routine, the days kind of run into each other). Then I think about what my plan is for the day, and what I'm going to eat for breakfast. This is all under my control and distracts me from thinking about all the things I'm unable to do as we are still in the midst of the pandemic. During the day, I remind myself multiple times what I am grateful for and look forward to seeing my children every Saturday on Zoom and my mother, brother, and sister weekly on Skype. In between, I reach out and message my PLN on Twitter and FB, and I send Whatsapp messages to friends I haven't heard from in a while just to check on them. I listen when they're upset, worried, or anxious and send words of kindness and compassion, so they know I've heard them. If they ask, I offer advice. I believe that's my role right now as I navigate my retirement which was supposed to be filled with travel to visit family and friends. It's much more constructive if I spend my time helping others find their way to well-being which makes me feel so much better.

SELF-BELONGING FOR TEACHERS

Created by: Dr. Ilene Winokur

Goal/Outcome:	**Connection to Belonging:**
Journey to your self-belonging and find your strengths, passions, and purpose by first awakening your self-awareness.	Knowing your strengths, passions, and purpose increases your sense of self-belonging

You're a busy educator supporting others: your family, your students, your colleagues, your friends. It's hard to make time for yourself. You know self-care is important, but what does that look like? The secret to happy and healthy personal and professional relationships and well-being is self-belonging. Spread your wings and learn how to F.L.Y. (First, Love Yourself). Self-belonging is the first step to healthy and happy relationships, positive self-talk, and well-being.

When you become more self-aware, you have an opportunity to explore your level of self-belonging and move forward on your journey to self-belonging. Your journey includes building your self-confidence, self-efficacy, self-esteem, self-worth, self-acceptance, and self-love. Starting your journey entails listing, either on paper or mentally, all that you have accomplished in your life, personally and professionally. Celebrate your accomplishments. Keep one or two in mind and remind yourself any time you experience self-doubt, imposter syndrome, or negative self-talk. For more about learning to

F.L.Y. (First, Love Yourself), register for my course on EduSpark.

The link is available on my website:
https://www.ilenewinokur.com/professional-development-with-ilenewinokur

CONNECTIONS AND GROWING YOUR SENSE OF BELONGING

Created by: Barbara Bray

Objective/Outcome:	Connection to Belonging:
Learn to tell your story by finding your purpose, your WHY	Making connections with others who share your purpose adds to your feelings of belonging.

We are social beings. During the pandemic, connections changed because we had to self-isolate, wear masks, and physically distance ourselves even from our families. This isolation and imposed distancing caused personal distress and changed what a sense of belonging meant during this crisis. After some thought about this, I wanted to consider how I got to that sense of belonging before the crisis.

RENTING SOMEONE ELSE'S STORY

When I was raising my children, I worked as a dental hygienist. Great job with good money. I could work part-time and raise my children. Yet, I didn't have that feeling I belonged. I went into the field because my guidance counselor told me I should apply. I did and was accepted into the program because of her story for me. I loved the people I worked with and had loyal patients who wanted to just see me but I didn't feel it was for me. I went back to school and became a dental hygiene instructor at the local college for four years. I also worked at my kids' school teaching after-school programs. I learned everything I could about computers and set up and ran the computer lab. I taught the Gifted and Talented classes, and adult computer classes, became a Chapter leader for the Young Astronauts, and more. I felt like I belonged, yet I was conflicted because I didn't want to give up my job as a hygienist.

DENTAL FLOSSING TO MENTAL FLOSSING

One night, I tripped and fell off my deck that was under construction. I broke my leg and damaged my neck. As I recuperated, I realized I was living my counselor's story instead of my own. After I healed, I believed it was time for me to live my life on purpose.

It was scary to start my life over at 40. Then I found my age didn't matter because the educators I met welcomed me with open arms. I joined East Bay CUE (formerly Computer Using Educators) and was part of a cohort through CTAP (California Technology Assistance Project) to build my skills. I learned how to write and groom grants and supported schools across the region. I also started teaching kids and teachers. I LOVED IT. I finally felt like I was getting closer to my purpose. Kids were excited about learning as we showcased the process and products. I started meeting educators from all over California at CUE Conferences and was asked to present what I learned.

BEING A CONNECTOR

One conference stood out and impressed me that I was a connector. I was walking down an intersection in an aisle when a librarian I knew showed up. We started talking. Another librarian I knew came up to say hi and didn't know the other librarian. I introduced them. Then another librarian I knew walked up. I introduced her to the others. As they started talking, I saw the AHA moments jump from one to the other. I walked away smiling. I felt like this was my purpose: to connect people with similar passions, ideas, roles, etc. I started a group on YahooGroups in the early 90s with over 400 educational technology geeks like me. We didn't have pictures on our profiles then, yet the connections grew and blossomed. I was stretching my reach and decided to go to the ISTE (International Society of Technology in Education) conferences. At one of the early ISTE conferences I attended, I was in the hotel elevator with another woman I didn't know. Neither of us were wearing our conference badges. She asked me where I was from and I said Oakland, California. She said, "I have a good friend from Oakland. We met on social media. Do you know Barbara Bray?" I answered with a big smile, "I'm Barbara." She then said, "I'm Janice from Missouri." We hugged and have been friends ever since.

STORIES CONNECT ALL OF US

As part of several grants, I was asked to lead multiple projects to support teachers in integrating technology across the curriculum. I helped write technology plans and visited schools all over the states and several other countries including Russia. In 1993, I started a Women's Ed Tech Consortium and set up retreats to connect and support one other. In 1997, I was asked to co-write the technology coordinator's column for CUE. In 2000, I became the sole writer for the professional development column. My first assignment was to get the stories from educators at ISTE in Atlanta, GA. I walked up to people I didn't know and just asked for their stories. I also asked people for names of people who inspire them and if they would connect me to them. I treasure that issue with the 12 stories and still have several of the connections I made then. I continued writing the column until 2014. I kept the past issues and read a few of the stories where I had interviewed different educators. The stories were good. I realized that I always loved the stories.

In 2017, I started the "Rethinking Learning" podcast to talk to inspirational thought leaders. I wanted to find out about their backstories and many shared stories they never told anyone before. I also made sure each podcast had a blog post to take each story deeper. The stories connected us. The stories fueled my passion and led me to my purpose.

CONNECTING AND BUILDING A SENSE OF BELONGING

That same year, I was at the Digital Badge Summit before the ISTE Conference and sat down at a table where a woman was sitting alone. I told myself to make sure no one sits alone. We started talking. Her story was amazing. I wanted to learn more about her, about Ilene Winokur. We talked about belonging and doing what we love. We ended up talking all night. Since this was her first ISTE, I saw that sparkle in her eyes when we talked about purpose and passion. We continued talking all the way through the ISTE conference where I introduced her to everyone I could. We were silly and serious. We've connected and roomed together at conferences and have been good friends ever since.

During the Covid pandemic, we continued to connect through Zoom. I did several podcasts over Zoom with Ilene. We are continuing to do virtual sessions together. When you meet people who really know you, and you know them, you feel that sense of belonging. That's how I felt and still feel with Ilene. We call ourselves soul sisters. It's like we've known each other forever. When you feel you have a purpose and are passionate about that purpose, you need to talk about it. I feel so fortunate that I can reach out to my soul sister to talk about any questions, concerns, ideas, and my purpose. This gives me a real sense of belonging.

FEELING EMPOWERED
Created by: Kristina Holzweiss

Goal/Outcome:	Connection to Belonging:
Teachers learn about the power to empower themselves and their students.	During the 26 years I have been educating children and adults, I have found that the key to helping people feel a sense of belonging all stems from empowerment. When we feel empowered, we feel that what we say and do matters.

Here are some ways that teachers can empower others:

1. *Roll out the red carpet.* The most important step in empowering others is to make them feel welcome. In her famous article, *Mirrors, Window, and Sliding Glass Doors,*[2] published in 1990, Dr. Rudine Sims Bishop used the phrase "windows, mirrors, and sliding glass doors" to explain the importance of children being able to see themselves and how they can learn about others through books. This idea is not only important in our classrooms, but also in our social environments. We must be aware that others will have different values and opinions based on their experiences and their backgrounds. We must make all people feel welcome, respected, and valued regardless of our differences. We must pay attention to signage in our classrooms, the

verbiage of our social media posts and written language, and our conversations. We must connect, not alienate.

2. *On a good day, I teach, on a great day I learn.* As an ed-tech librarian, I am excited when I experience a learner's "aha moment," that special time when their eyes light up because they discover something new, or overcome an obstacle. You can almost feel the synergy between teaching and learning. For an educator, this is the ultimate experience because you have helped someone change. They will never be the same, and this change will have an impact on all of their students. But it doesn't need to end here. When a person is empowered, they are able to give back. Take a moment during or at the end of your lesson or professional development session to learn from your students and colleagues. It could be about the skill or tool that you just taught them or about something that they chose. This completes the circle of giving and receiving so that everyone has the opportunity to grow from the experience. In my library program, I created a "Techspert" program where students could assist their classmates with using our makerspace equipment including our VR goggles, robots, and even the 3D printer! When students serve as support to their teachers, it helps them to develop leadership skills needed for their lives and future careers.

3. *We are better together.* Researchers have found that emperor penguins will take turns being warmed by

and warming others in their colony. Once an emperor penguin has been warmed up, it will move to the perimeter to give others the chance to enjoy the body heat in the inner circle. To welcome others into our professional learning network and classroom learning communities, we must create opportunities for our colleagues and students to develop teamwork while also celebrating individual contributions. During the pandemic, I established initiatives where my fellow librarians and educators could connect and shine. Using Book Creator, more than 30 librarians co-authored "The Digital Librarian's Survival Toolkit," and more than 50 educators co-authored "The Epic Ebook of Web Tools & Apps." These free ebooks were collaborative efforts and have freely been shared with the educational community worldwide. I also organized Edcamp Cardigan Camp, an Edcamp for librarians and other educators. There were almost 1,200 participants from all over the world during this day-long event of 64 discussions. Both opportunities were successful because educators came together for the greater good, while also sharing their particular expertise.

A STORY ABOUT BELONGING

Created by: Scott Nunes

Objective/Outcome:	Connection to Belonging:
Find your sense of self-belonging through self-exploration and discovery.	When you find your passion, your feelings of professional belonging increase.

Throughout my life, there have been times I felt I belonged. For most of my childhood, I'd say I found places to belong in school, in sports, and in my family. As I grew older that began to change; there were times I had to work to fit in or make a shift of where I belonged.

Professionally, for most of my life, I was an outsider. I was hated for my drive, ideas, and desire to make things better. Some employers made me jump through copious hoops before hearing out an idea. Others stripped my name from ideas and implemented them without attribution or acknowledgment of their true origin. In both circumstances ostracizing me was commonplace. This presented quite a challenge for me, and after some time I lost my drive and ambition. I began to believe some of the lies I was told. For example, I began to believe that my hard work and efforts were not enough or that I lacked the capacity to do extraordinary things. The foundation for change started about the time I got into education and was introduced to Dr. Carol Dweck's work on developing and maintaining a growth mindset. I set some long 4-6 year-long goals and I was determined to see them through no matter what before giving up or pivoting. I lost my job as a graphic designer and wanted something that was a bit more recession-proof. I set out to try my hand at education because for years people I knew and met through coaching would tell me I should get into education. They said I'd be great at it. I had no idea at the time they'd be right!

I am grateful for their gentle and not-so-gentle pushes. My goal was to be one of the best teachers in a short amount of time. I was willing to do whatever it took within reason. My dad was a great model of hard work, tenacity, and determination. One of my most powerful memories of his example is him driving home with a nail in his knee from 90 minutes away to relieve the babysitter watching me. He was laser-focused on his mission to provide and care for his family. If his doctor had let him go to work, he would have gone the next day. Now while the extreme lengths were high risk and possibly could have been handled differently, he knew there was no one else to care for me. My dad did not take days off and would power through. I had many opportunities to see him perform scores of others in martial arts and his field of construction. Some of my peers wanted to be like Mike, but I wanted to be like my dad. I set out with that same focus and determination to see this profession through no matter what. I was not going to be one of those that left the profession after 5 years. Additionally, I sought to be one of the best in less time.

I had no idea what was in-store or that I would surpass my expectations. I started by etching my path in my teacher induction program. I did more, exceeded expectations, and played to my strengths--technology, and everything related to it. My background in graphic design and basic coding helped me a ton! Once I started teaching, I discovered I could swap tech help/knowledge for curriculum tips and help with mastering the educational system. I took on added responsibilities to fill needed extracurricular activities and if someone needed a period subbed for or an adjunct shift picked up, I was their guy. Thanks to advice from my mentor I gained in value among the faculty and when we rolled out the district's 1:1 tech initiative, I became the tech guy. I not only belonged but was valued. Like genuinely valued.

I developed some great relationships with my coworkers and the students. I knew I mattered and others saw and acknowledged my value. That never really happened professionally prior to education. I loved every bit of my early years at that site. It was perfect--really. I had everything I needed to grow, find my teaching style, and develop a sense of belonging. A couple of years in though I started to max out my local professional learning opportunities. I had done most of the Professional Development (PD) offered by my district and locally. I needed more. A book study on Blended Learning was kicking off. I was excited! We tore through the book pretty fast and I still wanted more. My department chair gave me a list of names to search on the internet. Immediately, I turned to online teacher blogs like Catlin Tucker's and was floored! Here was someone that was 90 minutes from me that was an all-star! She was the teacher I wanted to be! She got it! Catlin was revolutionizing what could be done in traditional classrooms without gobs of money. She had a pretty sweet Bring Your Own Device (BYOD) system that trumped a lot of what I was seeing with 1:1 devices.

I started to explore larger edtech conferences to feed my desire for more edtech and tried to get funding to get them, but I was unsuccessful. However patient endurance attains all things. I got presented with an opportunity to go to ISTE 2018 because someone bowed out at the last minute and said yes. I was not ready for all the people. It was overwhelming. I had a great time and learned a lot, but did not maximize what it could be. I did pick up a few Twitter followers and went from 2 to 8. I was still hungry for more. I desperately wanted to go to the Schoology Next conference that year; they had Catlin Tucker as the keynote speaker and it was in my state. I could not procure outside funding. I waited and waited for a glimmer of hope, but none came. The tickets sold out, they opened up 25 more spots, but then sold out again. I found myself still examining the session list the night before and calculating out-of-pocket expenses. I told my wife I still had this desire to go, and my gut was telling me something transformative was going to take place. I had no idea what that was, but it was eating at me. She encouraged me to go and get it out of my system. I booked everything at 10:30 pm that evening and drove to the airport at 1:30 am, left San Francisco for San Diego at 6 am, and hit the ground running upon my arrival.

Once I got to the conference, I checked in and found my first session. I was excited. So many of the people there knew one another, but they were very welcoming, and I learned a ton from the presenter Glenn Irvin about Gamification! A new world of possibilities opened up for me. As the conference went on I got to meet tons of new people and saw Catlin Tucker speak 3 times! Dreams were fulfilled! Two things were absolutely pivotal at that conference: Becoming active on Twitter and finding my tribe. Denise Shovelin, one of the Schoology Ambassadors, forced me to post on Twitter, create a profile with an image, and interact live with people, but also on Twitter. I left with 131 followers. I was over the moon excited! Thanks to a score of Schoology Ambassadors I was welcomed into session after session, social after social. I stayed up late and got up at dawn to spend as much time with them as I could. It was a blast! On the last night, there was a side celebration for Phil Pulley and I remember thinking "Wow, how is this happening? Is this real life?" I was amazed that I just met these people and they welcomed me like I was one of them. It meant a lot to hear positive feedback from them on my ideas and what I was doing in my district. Glen Irvin encouraged me to keep going and I did!

Fast forward a couple of years I doubled down on edtech, started a couple of podcasts, and added in 3D printing. I just crossed the 10K followers mark too! I find joy in helping encourage others, sharing what I know, and giving others a sense of belonging. I look for those with talents and highlight the heck out of them. To me belonging is finding your niche, growing and learning alongside others, finding value, and being valued all at the same time. Connecting with others on Twitter gave me that. I cannot imagine that my life would be as rich and fulfilling as it is now without that moment that hinged on a gut feeling back in 2018. What if I had not listened to it, what if I had not invested in myself? Things would be okay, but they would be vastly different. I am glad I said yes to myself and to something new. I still prefer to connect in person, but when I cannot or I am separated from those I have a connection with, like Ilene Winokur, I find belonging on Twitter and encourage you to follow me on my journey in education, tag me in a post, and let me know what you are up to. I hope to hear about your journey!

LESSONS AND ACTIVITIES TO MODEL BECOMING A GOOD ANCESTOR

What is a good ancestor? It is someone who leaves a legacy of kindness, love, peace, and giving. Bina Venkataraman, notes in her research, that there are three things we must do:

1. Imagine the future
2. Seek out and listen to the voices of the future
3. Leave an heirloom, not a legacy which is just a personal passion project

She says we should, "embrace a broader view of community and humanity in what we choose to pass along."[1]

Why you should think about being a good ancestor (Bina Venkataraman)

Note that the lessons and activities in this chapter have been formatted differently because they are more narrative in nature rather than fit into a lesson plan template.

The World's Largest Lesson website[2] is filled with ideas, lessons, videos, and other resources that connect the United Nations Sustainable Development Goals (SDGs) with classroom lessons that are practical, and the students get involved in finding solutions to the world's biggest problems. The SDGs were adopted by the General Assembly of the United Nations in 2015 as an extension of the Millenium Development Goals. There are 17 Goals in total and many overlaps such as Goal #1 "No Poverty" and Goal #4 "Quality Education." The Goals include social objectives and environmental goals to be reached by the year 2030. Students are able to feel connected to what they are learning in practical and positive ways when focusing on their goals. This sense of connection to their local community and the world boosts their motivation to learn the concepts necessary to complete the task or project. Using the SDGs is one way for students to become problem solvers and begin their journey of becoming a Good Ancestor.

The World's Largest Lesson (website)

The Algorithm of Apologies	
Created by: Melody McAllister	
Objective/Outcome: Students learn what it means when we say "I'm sorry." Students learn that words matter. Students put their voice and words to their emotions.	**Connection to Belonging:** Relationships rely on people feeling remorse and understanding how their words and actions affect others. Knowing when and how to apologize is a very important life skill.

Today, as I introduced my youngest two girls, second grade and kindergarten, to the words and world of coding, we focused on algorithms, step-by-step instructions that we program into computers or robots. Artificial Intelligence doesn't have a brain like we do. If we aren't clear or we leave steps out, the computer won't know what to do. Along with my oldest two children, who are in sixth and fourth grades, we thought of all the algorithms we perform for our daily lives. Then, I gave them a boxed cookie recipe and their assignment was to work together to make something delicious. We talked about the instructions that weren't there, like washing our hands, making sure the kitchen was clean, and cleaning up afterward. We're humans and we can do that, but even as humans we need to learn the routines first.

It got me thinking about the algorithms of apologies. For years we've been teaching our kids to say things like, "sorry for being mean" when they get into disagreements. We even tell them to accept apologies! Often we make our kids do this when they are still really angry and upset. So they say the words, "sorry" and "it's okay" when they're really not feeling sorry or ready to forgive.

In my children's book, the *I'm Sorry Story*[3] I try to help young people, and any person reading my book, to see that words like "sorry" or "it's okay" don't mean anything when we force our kids to apologize and forgive. Our intentions as parents and educators are very good. We want our children and students to learn how to take ownership of their mistakes and not unfriend every person they disagree with in life. We know that in order to be successful citizens, employees, and form successful relationships, we understand how important genuine apologies are in the grand scheme of life!

PROCESSING

However, maybe it's time to really take a look at the old algorithm. For instance, the practice of bringing two or more young people together after a fight or argument and we say, "Now tell them you're sorry." Wait, what if they aren't feeling sorry yet? Isn't that important? Yes! When I've talked to young people all over the world after reading my story, 100% of them know what it feels like to hear and say a forced apology.

They know when it's fake.

They agree it means nothing.

Let's allow for a cooling-off period. Let's throw in wait time. It could be an hour, a day, or whatever time it needs. Stealing a pencil or favorite Pokemon card might need thirty minutes of cooling downtime, but gossiping and telling lies about someone might need days or more.

In the meantime, let's talk with our young people. Let them tell us how they are feeling. Let them process the hurt, anger, and even guilt or remorse. Let's be non-judgemental and ask guiding questions (when appropriate) like "When ____happened, how did you respond?" "When ____happened, what emotion did you feel more of, anger, sadness, fear, confusion (etc.)?" Or "Now that ____ time has passed, how are you feeling?" or "How have your emotions changed?"

Whatever we ask our young people, we need to focus on questions that help them understand their emotions and actions without adding more guilt. Genuine emotions are not wrong or bad. I learned many years ago that natural stress regarding deadlines or getting paid helps us complete necessary jobs! In the same way, helping our young people feel their genuine emotions will help guide them to sincere apologies. OR NOT. My belief is that a fake apology is worse than no apology.

We can do the same for helping our students process forgiveness. They need to understand it's their choice. We need to help them understand that forgiveness is healing but it doesn't need to be hurried. Often we hear people say "it's okay" when someone apologizes, but it's not okay for people to hurt us, and when we force kids to "accept" apologies on a timeline that has not allowed them to process their true emotions, their response of "it's okay" is their way of appeasing us.

A BETTER ALGORITHM FOR APOLOGIES

The algorithm of apologies and forgiveness are as complex as we are. Helping young people put their voice and words to emotions is going to help them long-term, but forcing them to say what we want them to say when we want them to say it, doesn't do anything helpful in regards to learning how to process the sincerity of both actions. It also takes away their free will and grows people who are confused about why others aren't ready to accept their apologies or who were never really taught how to forgive and heal.

We can do better for our children and students. We can do better for all the people in our lives. One of the most important things we can add to the algorithm is time to process and be genuine. And beyond giving our students the proper words of apologies, the best way we can teach them this process is to model it with our own behavior. When we put more emphasis on the reality of hurting and healing, get away from rote words, and then show up with a genuine apology that truly helps another person heal, we've modeled something that is priceless. Consistently, over time, with our modeling and words to help their own process of emotions, we are giving our children and students a true-to-life lesson in genuine apologies and forgiveness.[4]

The Algorithm of Apologies (Melody McAllister)

PEACE AND JUSTICE LESSON

Created by: Bhavna Mathew

Objective/Outcome:	Connection to Belonging:
Inquiry-based lesson to coincide with the International Day of Peace	Students take ownership of their learning using inquiry and sparking their curiosity. A sense of belonging to the world at large is fostered through questioning, researching, and finding answers to difficult questions related to peace, social justice, and how we can make the world a better place for all.

Each year the International Day of Peace is observed around the world on the 21st of September. The UN General Assembly has declared this as a day devoted to strengthening the ideals of peace, through observing 24 hours of non-violence and cease-fire.

ACTIVITY/PROJECT DESCRIPTION:

The Weekly Plan/Lesson plan[5] is an outline for the educators to plan and manage their time, constructively. However, it should not restrict the Voice-Choice and ownership of a learner. It can be flexible and foster inquiry-based learning. It should empower the learners to become agents of their own learning. Make notes of their inquiry questions during the week which can be added by them on a wonder wall. This will help you to plan for next week, monitor their interest and spark their curiosity.

Wakelet collection with a lesson resources (Bhavna Mathew)

Build Your Personal Brand
Created by: Justin Nolan

Objective/Outcome:	Connection to Belonging:
This lesson teaches teens about the important concept of personal branding. It allows them to discuss brand building in general, learn the definition of personal branding, and start to build a brand of their own by reflecting on their values, goals, and dreams.	While building a personal brand, students see how they need to bring value to others. When we bring value to others, we learn to become a good ancestor.

1. Activation:

Choose one or more of the following activation activities. *If you do this lesson over multiple days, you could use a different one each day.

Activation A: "Post It Pile It"

- Tell students how the activity works first. Provide each student with a small pack of post-it notes. Tell the students that you are going to give them a topic, and they will record their word association responses to the question on post-it notes. They should write only one idea per note but will write down as many different ideas as they can.
- Read the following question to students:

What comes to mind when you think of the topic "building a company brand?"

- Tell the students to think silently about their answers (for 1 minute) writing one idea per post-it on their stack of post-it notes. They will keep all their post-it notes in front of them.
- Read the following question to students:

What comes to mind when you think of the topic "building a personal brand?"

Tell the students to think silently about their answers (for 1 minute) writing one idea per post-it on their stack of post-it notes. They will keep all their post-it notes in front of them.

- Place each post-it note in front of them and then discuss what they have written and if they have duplicates place them together in a pile.
- Put the word "BRAND BUILDING" on a large chart paper or board and ask for a volunteer to give one post-it reply. For example, NIKE, or Values
- Ask if anyone had a very similar answer and have all students place their post-its on the chart/board in the same place.
- Repeat this process until almost all posts have been organized on the poster. A fun optional activity is to keep this poster for the classroom wall.

Activation B: "Brainstorm Discussion"
Simply show your group the word "BRAND" and host a discussion about what that makes them think of.

Activation C: "Brand Samples"

To increase the depth of the discussion, show some logos of brands, or a commercial from a brand as a company, and host a discussion with your group as to what the word means.

2. Definitions of Brand Building:

After activation discussions, show and read a quote on branding to students (the following are two examples):

> *"A brand is simply a promise. It is the set of expectations, memories, stories and relationships that, taken together, account for a consumer's decision to choose one relationship, product or service over another."* (Seth Godin, author and business executive)

> *"Building a personal brand is important regardless of what you want to do. Creating your own personal brand through the professional experiences you've had and through the experiences and courses you've taken is important. I use various social networking tools to create a personal brand. Also, when I meet people physically, when I network with them, I always take care to tell them what I've done, why I'm relevant, and I tailor it to them."* (Tony Wang, Bioethicist and Fashion Blogger)

3. Read & Respond. What is a personal brand?
Read aloud, individually, or in groups, the article "10 Golden Rules Of Personal Branding" (Goldie Chan)

Have students write down:

A. One connection to the real world
B. One connection to their personal life
C. One new thing they learned
D. One question it made them think about

** Submit answers or host a reflection discussion quickly

4. Projects. Use one or more of the following activities to showcase learning in an active, creative, and potentially creative way.

Using the resource B. You Are The Brand: Brand Design Questions there are a number of ways to create projects.

Personal Or Partner Activity. You have the choice as a leader to use this for collaboration, or individual projects, but using the resource *B. You Are The Brand: Brand Design Questions*:

Have students interview each other, or answer the questions individually.

If you would like it to be creative, there are many options. Students could use the information gathered to:

i. Make a fake or real social media profile.

ii. Create a promotional poster for the brand.

iii. Write an acceptance speech for a lifetime achievement award.

RESOURCES:

A. 10 Golden Rules Of Personal Branding by Goldie Chan

Creating a personal brand can be a daunting, mythical task. And one of the easiest ways to get lost in the process is to not know where to start. Even Oprah Winfrey began by going through several style iterations on a small local show before defining her voice into one of the most influential personal brands in the world.

In both our look-at-me cultural shift and evolving job market, it's both helpful and necessary to stand out when applying for a job or starting your own company. A personal brand is for (almost) everyone. So here are 10 golden rules for creating an engaging, unique, and inviting personal brand.

1. Have a focus.
"Too many people are unfocused when it comes to press and coverage, trying to be "everything to everyone." Decide what your key message is and stick to it," says Cooper Harris, founder, and CEO of Klickly. Her personal brand has undergone a dramatic shift—from working actress to respected tech entrepreneur and she has handled this shift by only

focusing on one message at a time. Keeping your message focused on your target demographic will make it that much easier to both create content around your personal brand and have others define you.

In fact, Adam Smiley Poswolsky, millennial workplace expert and author of *The Breakthrough Speaker*, takes it one step further when he's advising speakers: "Carve a niche and then carve a niche within your niche. The best personal brands are very specific." And Juan Felipe Campos, VP of tech and partner at Manos Accelerator, goes one step further to focus on communities that he targets with his large-scale clients. "Keep your message and content consistent to one niche topic to become memorable within a targeted community." The narrower and more focused your brand is, the easier it is for people to remember who you are. And when it comes time to hire a speaker or a new employee, your narrowed-down brand will be what they remember.

2. Be genuine.

There's an easy way to have an original personal brand—and that is to be genuine and authentic. Millennial influencer and head of marketing at Popular Demand, Monica Lin, says, "People can see right through a disingenuous act." The more obviously a brand is a copycat, the more the audience will call out the perpetrator for it. Monica's personal brand experienced a huge amount of growth after she began engaging with her audience more meaningfully on Twitter.

"Be genuine. It will make it much easier to manage your personal brand on a daily basis," explained William Harris, Facebook ads expert at Element. Your personal brand should be an easy daily filter that you create content and reach out to your audience with. And finally, Justin Wu, founder of CoinState says "Be a master of your craft, skillset or industry before starting a personal brand. Then your content will help amplify who you are." When initially building his personal brand, he garnered a reputation of being an expert in his field while simultaneously amplifying on social media that same renown. If you're deeply skilled in one area, your reputation alone will help you build the brand you want.

3. Tell a story.

If your personal brand isn't telling a story, you've already lost half of your potential audience. Allen Gannett, chief strategy officer at Skyword and author of *The Creative Curve* explains it best. "The most effective personal branding strategy these days is to build a true narrative - single character monologues are boring in Tinseltown, and even more boring for your personal brand."[6] No one wants to hear you shout about your brand into the social media void, so create a story around your brand that your audience can engage with. Allen regularly meets and chats with his audience in airports around the world, further developing his warm and friendly personal brand.

One of the best ways to tell that story is through written content or video. For Pelpina Trip, a social video strategist, this is definitely the case. Her own video channel on LinkedIn sees some of the highest levels of engagement across the platform. "The most personal way to communicate online is with video. Simply use your smartphone to video message your clients, make a personal connection with prospective clients and connect with co-workers. After all, you always have your smartphone on you!"

4. Be consistent.

Being consistent is very similar to having a narrow focus.It's much easier to get recognized for one topic if you consistently create content and brand voice around it. "Ensure that your personal brand promise stays consistent, both online and offline," explains Fyiona Yong, director and millennial leadership coach (ICF ACC). She regularly works with millennials in a corporate context to help them define their more conservative work goals. "You have to demonstrate consistency across your communication, gravitas, and appearance. Don't underestimate how tiny inconsistencies can derail personal brand effectiveness." On the opposite, creative side, CyreneQ, a top storyteller on Snapchat, suggests "something consistent either visually or personality-wise. Something unique that people can associate with your brand and know it's you. For example, a sidekick mascot or having a catchphrase you say after every video - something people can fall in love with." Her sidekick mascot, Ele, has garnered millions of views per Snap for brand work, allowing her fun personal brand to represent big box brands like Walmart and DC. So whether you're creating a wild, incredibly out-there fun brand or one that's a bit more on the conservative, the corporate side, consistency is key.

5. Be ready to fail.

Failure is tough, and all of us generally want to avoid it because that's human nature. However, to have a personal brand that rises above the rest, you need to have a failure. Walt Disney spoke of this often when he reminisced about his failed first attempts at creating an animation brand. "I think it's important to have a good hard failure when you're young. I learned a lot out of that. Because it makes you kind of aware of what can happen to you." And what can happen is never as frightening as not trying at all.

When Timothy Hoang, CEO of Stories By Tim, Inc. develops his influencer clients, he likes to tell them: "You'll never achieve the best branding until you fail a couple of times while pushing past your comfort zone." The very best brands always come from repeated trial and error, mistakes and failures, and not from instant perfection.

6. Create a positive impact.

After you've developed your personal brand over a period of time, there are generally two ways to continue to build your brand. You can hop over others and burn bridges or steadily grow a community around your brand. Jacob Shwirtz, head of social partnerships at WeWork, who has worked with many of the top influencers in the world, including makeup personality, Michelle Phan, gives us this wisdom.

My quick tip on personal branding is to remember you are your brand, no matter what your current job is, what project you happen to be working on at any one time, or whatever the priority happens to be today... always keep in mind the impact you leave on others and remember all we have is our own reputation and that's our brand, so be awesome to each other! Keeping a positive attitude and helping others will only help healthily grow your brand in the long run.

7. Follow a successful example.
"People interested in personal branding need to start marketing themselves like the celebrities and influential people that they look up to every day," explains Jason Wong, CEO of Wonghaus Ventures. His own personal brand has gone viral several times, over subjects like ice cream in Japan, inflatable pool toys, and memes, earning him the title of the "Meme King." His success often comes from studying trends and popular individuals on different social media platforms and then implementing them with a twist. Creatively dissecting social analytics and establishing the next big trend can be within your grasp too, if you pay attention across all social media platforms and not simply focus narrowly on one of them.

8. Live your brand.
As mentioned before, one of the ways you can make building a personal brand difficult for yourself is to separate your brand from your personal life. While certainly doable, it's easier when

initially creating a personal brand to have your actual lifestyle and brand be one and the same.

Tim Salau, community builder and founder of Mentors & Mentees, who works with college students to help them build brands that will get them hired, believes in this idea as well. "Your personal brand should follow you everywhere you go. It needs to be an authentic manifestation of who you are and amplify what you believe." With this in mind, your personal brand is not only a reflection of a series of job functions like marketing, finance, or creativity but also ideals like giving back thoughtful leadership or mentorship.

9. Let other people tell your story.

The best PR is by word of mouth. Creating a personal brand in the public sphere is no exception to this rule. Aaron Orendorff, editor in chief at Shopify Plus, tells his personal story through lively videos and the occasional bunny co-host or two and his audience remembers. They're able to recall the bright outfits and the animal friends and tie those pieces of the story to their interpretation of his brand. As he eloquently states: "Personal branding is the story people tell about you when you're not in the room." Jessie Maltin, co-host of Maltin On Movies works with her father, renowned film critic Leonard Maltin, and has watched him build his career over the past several decades. "All you have in your life is your name and the reputation you garner."

10. Leave a legacy.

Once you've built your personal brand with a reputation and community behind it, the next step is to think about the legacy that you'll leave behind. What are the keywords and actions that you want to be known for? Blake Jamieson, artist at Blake Jamieson LLC, who paints pop art portraits of famous tech and sports heroes reminds us that: "Building a personal brand is much bigger than building a business. The only exit strategy is legacy."

A personal brand is a lifelong project that constantly evolves and changes. Even the experts who build or enhance the biggest brands in the business know that there are no hard-set rules for creating a personal brand. But these general guidelines help provide first steps, especially if you're starting a new brand or rebranding.

Creating the right personal brand will not only help you be known in your field and consistently land work but it could be the difference between "Who are you?" and "Thank you for being here" in your career.

B. You Are The Brand: Brand Design Questions

Developing a personal brand requires self-awareness and assessment of values, goals, and dreams, as well as a sense of how others see you. Use these questions to determine the overall scope of any personal brand.

1. What are your personal values that are important to you?
2. What are your favorite things to learn about? Why?
3. Describe some of your interests. What kind of things are you involved in?
4. What are two strengths you possess and describe a time when these strengths contributed to your success?
5. Describe one of your greatest accomplishments.
6. What do you see yourself doing in the future? What are some goals and dreams you have?
7. What is a quote you live by?

EPILOGUE

I believe it is fitting to end this workbook with "Building Your Brand." Why? Because our "brand" is our reputation. It's who we are authentically. It is the legacy we leave for others who come after us and our tribute to those who laid the groundwork for us.

Finding Your Pathway to Belonging in Education is intended to be a guide to spark your ideas for lessons and activities that will instill a sense of safety and belonging in your classroom, your school, and the wider community. Find what works for you and your students, then modify, have fun with, and enjoy learning more about yourself, your colleagues, and your students. Feel empowered, confident, and support others on their journeys to belonging.

I want to thank all of the educators who contributed their lessons and activities to this book. When I put out the call for contributions, there were so many amazing educators who raised their hands. Be sure to reach out to them on social media. My goal for this book is to expand on my first book, *Journey to Belonging: Pathways to Well-Being*, by showing how easy it is to change the culture in your classroom and your school to be more inclusive, equitable, welcoming, and create safe spaces within diverse communities that support brave conversations. I know there are many other ways besides the lessons and activities in this book to instill a sense of belonging in your classroom. It would be awesome for YOU to share something you're doing that supports your students sense of belonging. Post it on social media and tag me (@ilenewinokur) and #Journey2Belonging.

I wrote in my first book that I was in my mid-thirties before I started my journey to belonging. It's imperative that our children and our students shouldn't have to wait that long. In fact, I have chatted with people who are still searching for their sense of belonging well into their 50s and 60s. My hope is that reading through this workbook and using the activities and lessons will support your professional belonging journey and will, in turn, support your students' journeys to belonging.

ADDITIONAL RESOURCES

https://
journeys2belonging.
com/3o9iAYr

This Wakelet collection will be updated regularly with the latest articles, blog posts, podcast episodes, and videos for finding your pathway and starting your journey to belonging. It is exclusively for those who have purchased or been gifted this book, so the link should not be shared with anyone. Check back regularly to find new items. The collection also includes other collections I have created including, *Creating a Sense of Belonging in Your Classroom* and *Othering and Gender Identity.*

NOTES

HOW TO USE THIS BOOK

1. For more about backward design: https://cft.vanderbilt.edu/guides-sub-pages/understanding-by-design

CREATING A SAFE AND WELCOMING ENVIRONMENT FOR ALL

1. https://journeys2belonging.com/3IyL6KY
2. https://journeys2belonging.com/3g24CTM

LESSON PLANNING AND INSTILLING A SENSE OF BELONGING

1. https://journeys2belonging.com/3fVNdfn

AN ASSET-BASED APPROACH TO TEACHING

1. https://journeys2belonging.com/3u2hLVa
2. https://journeys2belonging.com/3G4o1y3

LESSONS AND ACTIVITIES FOR SELF-BELONGING

1. https://journeys2belonging.com/3fVV8JF

INCLUSIVE PRACTICES FOR LANGUAGE LEARNERS

1. https://journeys2belonging.com/3EqyEhB
2. WIDA 2020 standards pdf in ELL Wakelet collection (see #6)
3. https://journeys2belonging.com/3FUytIo
4. https://journeys2belonging.com/3Apxted
5. https://wke.lt/w/s/h4iPyl
6. https://journeys2belonging.com/3Iv95dH
7. https://journeys2belonging.com/3rNQfrG
8. https://journeys2belonging.com/340ISF2
9. https://journeys2belonging.com/3g095Gp
10. https://journeys2belonging.com/3o4i2Dc
11. https://journeys2belonging.com/340ISF2

LESSONS AND ACTIVITIES FOR PROFESSIONAL BELONGING

1. https://journeys2belonging.com/3yoL1F0
2. https://journeys2belonging.com/3C2YlBV

LESSONS AND ACTIVITIES TO MODEL BECOMING A GOOD ANCESTOR

1. https://journeys2belonging.com/3AAWl2w
2. https://journeys2belonging.com/3KwKhUy
3. https://journeys2belonging.com/3rJMe7I
4. https://journeys2belonging.com/3WkihIZ
5. https://wke.lt/w/s/JB0b9k
6. https://journeys2belonging.com/3V2uaC6

ABOUT THE AUTHOR

Dr. Ilene Winokur has lived in Kuwait since 1984 and is a professional development specialist supporting teachers globally including refugee teachers. Ilene has been active in learning innovation for over 25 years, is an expert in professional development, and passionate about narratives related to belonging. Prior to retiring in 2019, she was a teacher and administrator at the elementary and pre-college levels in Kuwait and specialized in ESL. Her blog, podcast, and books focus on the importance of feeling a sense of belonging. Ilene strongly believes in bringing communities together with her focus on professional belonging; learning and collaborating in a professional setting. You can connect with Ilene on Twitter @IleneWinokur and find links to her podcast and blog on her website https://www.ilenewinokur.com

EduMatch

PUBLISHING